Listening
for Truth

Praying Our Way
to Virtue

James Keating

Liguori
ONE LIGUORI DRIVE
LIGUORI MO 63057-9999

Imprimi Potest:
Richard Thibodeau, C.Ss.R.
Provincial, Denver Province
The Redemptorists

ISBN 0-7648-0816-8
Library of Congress Catalog Number: 2001092240

Scripture quotations are from the *New Revised Standard Version of the Bible*, copyright © 1989 by the Division of Christian Education of the National Council of Churches of Christ in the USA. Used with permission. All rights reserved.

To order, call 1-800-325-9521
www.liguori.org
www.catholicbooksonline.com

Dedication

*To Ina Mairead, a blessing beyond all telling,
and to all women who faithfully work
the fields of Christian motherhood, praying
and hoping for a harvest of saints
in their children, especially Kris Gehring,
Rita McCabe, Toni Mitchell,
and, of course, Marianne.*

ᕽ

Contents

Introduction

Prayer, whether offered as an individual or as a community in a liturgical setting, is the seeking of communion with God. The moral life also seeks communion, but its first purpose is to facilitate communion with what is *morally* good, not with what is *ultimately* good, namely, God. But the two are not opposed in any way. In fact, the more one grows in moral goodness the more one seeks completion in what is ultimate. Being good, in other words, is *not* its own reward; the virtuous may come to a certain sense of peace in their dispositions and behavior, but their "hearts are still restless until they rest in God" (Saint Augustine).

We are made for "more" than virtue, but we cannot enjoy that "more"—which has been identified by faith as communion with God—without first attaining moral goodness. If we were to come to God first, without seeking moral goodness, God would lead us to virtue. Coming to God through a *religious conversion* is simply the implicit beginning of a *moral conversion*, just as coming to *moral conversion* is the beginning of communing with the ultimate source of all virtue: God. Thus, prayer (discovering and communing with God) and virtue (being faithful to the meaning of what is morally good) complete and define one another. Their joining together *explicitly* in every Christian life and community is *the way* to enter the struggle of *taking on* virtue even as one *accepts the gifts* to "put on the Lord Jesus Christ" (Romans 13:14). In other words, living in prayer and virtue places us at the very core of discipleship.

There are thousands of descriptions of prayer in thousands, maybe millions, of books and essays. What characterizes my approach in this book, however, is that I am going to describe prayer from a perspective of growing in moral virtue. Of course, prayer cannot be manipulated for our ends, but like communication with one's spouse, it can *serve the purpose* of deepening communion with your beloved regardless of the specific topic at hand. It is the communication itself that serves to deepen intimacy, not the content of the message. One can grow in communion with a spouse even while speaking about mundane domestic issues as long as the spouse is attended to in love and respect. Similarly, if we converse with God in faith and hope and love about any topic, we will grow in intimacy with God. Certainly, we are concerned with our growth in moral goodness; our very "success" as a human person is at stake in becoming good. God is equally concerned with that topic for our sake, and so we can approach God and converse about our need for moral conversion.

CHAPTER ONE

Prayer, A Basic Christian Need

C hristian moral living appears at once lofty and yet ordinary. Many Christians report how frustrated they are with their perceived lack of growth in virtue. The moral life seems unattainable. It is mentioned by some that they carry their struggle with pride for decades, or the burdens of lust or greed have weighed them down year after year. For others, envy gnaws away at their inner peace and refuses to yield to the development of steady and pacific virtues. Yet, in spite of personal failure and struggle, many of us do not give up on moral growth and yield to cynicism. We want to believe we can reach a place in life where temptation is muted, even if not eradicated; a place where we make decisions out of the hope and knowledge of being persons who possesses a dignity from God. Do we ever reach a place of such rest and strength?

The answer to that is, as to most things human, yes and no. We can reach a place where, for the most part, our decisions are the fruit of dispositions yielded over to God in faith, hope, and love. But there will be a remainder factor. This factor is the *struggle* to be good; the *work* of remembering our dignity and living accordingly; the *task* of being focused upon fidelity when many around us, and voices within us, tempt us to go lower rather than higher. I am using the words *struggle, work,* and *task* not to reduce moral living to simply an exercise in will power, but rather to contextualize it in our real life-graced efforts to do the right thing.

Simply saying that moral living is a grace, or to encourage the struggling ones to "lighten up" in their quest for virtue, may in fact be just that: too simple. We recognize that emotional and mental pathologies and various neurotic tendencies can heighten the anxiety or impossibility of such persons achieving moral peace. Of course, noting this does not end the reality of struggle for those who are balanced, sane, and integrated. The most fruitless choice is to try to end the struggle by giving in to the temptation. Trying to end the struggle by giving in to the unrelenting gnawing of envy, for example, certainly takes some pressure off, but only in the way abuse of alcohol relieves the pressure to escape a truth too real to bear: It masks an unpleasant reality, it doesn't remove it. Giving in to a vice merely quiets the voice of temptation long enough for one to engage in the object of such temptation. After the morbid delight is satisfied, we find that the voice of temptation has not gone away satisfied and full. Rather, the tempting vice takes up residence in us, and it will not leave if we continue to yield to its voice; in fact, just the opposite, it comes to possess us. To arrive at such a state is the true origin of personal horror. Becoming morally good does involve a struggle—in due proportion, a struggle that hopes to break the bonds to vice we have built up over the years.

Therefore, since we are surrounded by so great a cloud of witnesses, let us also lay aside every weight and the sin that clings so closely, and let us run with perseverance the race that is set before us, looking to Jesus the pioneer and perfecter of our faith, who for the sake of the joy that was set before him endured the cross, disregarding its shame, and has taken his seat at the right hand of the throne of God. Consider him who endured such hostility against himself from sinners, so that you may not grow weary or lose heart. In your struggle against sin you have not yet resisted to the point of shedding your blood.

HEBREWS 12:1-4

The writer of Hebrews reminds us that sin is to be struggled against—a struggle so important that we should go to the point of death rather than sin gravely. In a culture wherein the meaning of sin has been blunted, and our presumptions lie in the realm of *God's love* covering a multitude of *our sins*, the idea of dying rather than sinning appears quaint or even dangerous. The Church's ministry needs to recover a relevant theology of sin for our age, one that highlights sin's power to destroy intimacy with God due to our actions. Of course God loves us. The question that needs to be asked again and again is, do we love God? Do we express this love in the only way open to humankind—moral behavior?

The horror of living an unethical life is the pain of knowing that the vicious person I have become is, in part, what I chose to become. The horror is that, in listening to the voice of temptation, I close myself within my self—and end up with *only* myself. But not my *best* self, not my real, dignified self; only an aspect of myself, one that comes from a broken part of me, a desire loose and unruly. It is somewhat like receiving a medical diagnosis that portends a heart attack, and realizing that my choices of diet and lack of exercise have actually brought it on. This physical condition did not *just happen* to me; I created the conditions necessary for it to be present in me. I ask, "Why didn't I heed all the advice given about heart disease earlier and so avoid my present state?" Part of the horror is my own complicity. The truth comes crashing in—it really didn't have to be this way. My choices facilitated my present condition. And so it is with moral evil. The development of a moral character bent on vice is not seen as real or relevant to *my* life. Evil cannot touch *me.*

Just as we contribute to our own premature physical death through choices that ignore the reality of food and sloth's effect upon the body, so we contribute to the soul's death by ignoring the fact that our willed actions create a spiritual character that is immortal. For good or for ill, we are becoming who we choose to be—in cooperation with grace and truth or against them. In today's western culture, the primary struggle may not be in our efforts to overcome evil's temptations, but in simply coming to recognize the fact that our choices matter in the coming-to-be of our ever-lasting identity. As one evangelist put it, the problem today is not saving people's souls, but helping them to see that they have one!

Fidelity to moral living demands a certain fighting spirit. The way *out* of this oppressive struggle with evil, however, is the way *through* the door of virtue. This doorway leads to a life of becoming good, understood as task and gift, struggle and grace. We grow in virtue by living faithfully our vocation. Becoming good is both task and gift within the ordinariness of living out our vocation. But where does the *gift* of living *virtuously* come from? Who is our *donor* in the realm of *virtue*?

Meditation Room:

The virtue of *honesty* bids us to look at our choices
and character clearly despite the pain of self-examination. Do
you really love God, and do you express this love
in worship and moral action?

God as Enabler of Virtue

The struggle to be good and our rush from the horror of our own sin and moral failure is met eagerly by God in the unleashing of God's many gifts. We are called to be faithful to God's vision of our exalted dignity. God wants us to access divine power in order to turn our heart and mind from self or self-hate alone, to "abundant" life (John 10:10). Only in the interpenetration of moral living and spiritual living will the full power of Christian moral conversion be experienced. This full power is known when our desire to be good is met with the gifts of the Holy Spirit.

This aligning of the moral with the *spiritual* fully opens the human quest for virtue to the divine will for our salvation. Our longing to be good is met with God's desire to call us into holiness, into a sharing in God's own life. Our destiny is communion with God and all the saints, thus every *spiritual help* is ours to draw from in order to reach this divinely ordained goal. Even so, the *struggle* of becoming virtuous may loom large in our imaginations. The fear of what we may have to go through to become good is enough to give us pause and "count the cost." We think, in other words, that it would be better if we could "magically" experience God meeting us with salvific desire. In reality, this desire of God's to save us through Jesus Christ is not the end of moral struggle, but its grounding and reordering toward its proper goal: "the heavenly call of God in Christ Jesus" (Philippians 3:14). There will be miracles on occasion (they are rare—that is one of the reasons they are miracles), but there will be no magic. There will, in other words, be no easy way to appropriate our own growth in self-knowledge and knowledge of God, which is the very stuff of life. Oddly enough, if we were to be "saved" from that measured growth, life would be unbearably boring.

Thus, we need to investigate what it means to be in communion with God while developing moral virtue. To understand this communion is to understand the very core of what it means to live in faith and hope and love. The immense depth of such communion is, in fact, the very fabric of the Christian religion itself, and so, in order to focus a bit, I will offer a facet of this mystery of virtue and spirituality through the experience of prayer.

Meditation Room:

Recall a time when an ordinary *conversation* with your spouse or friend secured a deeper bond of love between you.

What does prayer look like when it is ushered into service as a facilitator of moral virtue? I will call this kind of prayer "virtue prayer." One characteristic of virtue prayer is that it is petitionary, and yet it is also a cry for moral goodness founded upon contemplation. Further, virtue prayer encompasses both personal and liturgical expressions; it stands as incomplete without this rhythm.

Virtue prayer, then, is at heart a form of contemplative prayer that expresses our eager longing to be good and holy. Through virtue prayer, we become more vulnerable to moral goodness while trying to reach the presence of all goodness: God. We desire to know God, who is all good, in order to share in the divine goodness. In this prayer, there is a yearning to be *one* with God, to be *like* God, to be a *friend* of God. And it is when this yearning is satisfied in prayerful union with God that such a union becomes the well of virtue. From out of such friendship with God comes a certain knowledge of moral goodness and the strength to act upon that knowledge.

By saying "the knowledge of moral goodness," I do not mean to suggest that we always get right answers to moral dilemmas from simply praying. For believers, the entire search for what is morally good encompasses a disposition to be open to God in truth. This search, however, is made explicit in periods of prayer. Out of this kind of prayer, we also come to know what to ask of God in petitionary prayer, for within the personal conversations we have with God, in our depths, comes knowledge of our real moral needs.

Petitions regarding our own moral state, then, are the fruit of clearly seeing our self before the truth who is God (contemplation). In light of God's love and mercy, we see our real identity and come to know what we need to ask for in order to conform to our dignified identity as God's beloved. In other words, we come to know what virtues we are lacking, and we begin to trustingly place our vices into the merciful heart of Christ. From out of his Sacred Heart, Christ responds to our trust by enveloping our entire life in mercy and sending us a call to conversion. The beginning of moral wisdom is to rejoice in knowing that we have a personal need for conversion. Resistance to such a call is known as "hardness of heart" in the Scriptures (Jeremiah 11:8; 16:12). This hardness thwarts conversion, and blocks the joy of knowing what it is to be loved even as we are still in the midst of turning from vice to virtue.

In the light of acknowledging a need to convert from sin, we come to sense what our many struggles are and to bring this clear knowledge of who we are to prayer. Petitionary prayer, asking God for virtue, takes on an urgency. It is not a frantic urgency or a neurotic obsession with our own faults, but a firmness of purpose in the light of Christ's sure promise of mercy. We begin to see that vice cannot be overcome simply by good intentions and good will; vice has to be given over to God in Christ. As a result of this giving over in prayer, we can bear our own conversions. Otherwise, we would end up hating ourselves and despairing.

Bringing our sins to petitionary prayer can be done at any time during our day, but this kind of prayer takes on a special potency if uttered during Mass. In the Mass, we are participating in the very mystery of salvation—Christ's self offering upon the cross and his Resurrection. Here, at the very center of all conversions, it is best to bring our sins and lay them at Christ's feet for healing, forgiveness, and our own elevation into graced living.

In some sense, also, we can look upon the sacrament of reconciliation as a petitionary prayer. Here is the forum within which we can truly name the vices that hold us back from living a life of freedom in grace. We come to this sacrament to beg Christ to forgive us and sustain us in conversion. I use the word "beg," not because Christ is some kind of psychotic master who longs to see his servants grovel and plead; rather, I beg because *I come to see so clearly* how chained I am in my life of sin. I feel an urgency to come totally to Christ right now. *My own urgency* bids me to beg in the light of the destruction I have been shown, the consequences of my own sins.

Meditation Room:

**The virtue of *prudence* invites us to become persons
who insightfully know the correct means to correct goals.
What is the best means you know of to stabilize
your commitment to turn from sin?**

Having a knowledge of the negative effects of sin is essential to making a move from a life of vice to one of virtue. Let me illustrate this knowledge with an analogy.

Imagine a man has promised his wife he will call her before he returns home from a business trip. This phone call is vital to the wife because family plans depend upon the husband's time of return. Without knowing when he will return, she cannot properly arrange for the transportation of their children to band and sports practice. Further, the couple has an infant son and toddler whom the wife was hoping she would not have to take out into the winter weather in the course of driving the older children to their commitments. Whether she has to pack the entire family into the car in order to taxi the older children around depends upon her husband's time of return.

The husband decides not to call his wife. He reasons that he will make it home in time to take the children where they need to go. He vaguely remembers what time their commitments begin, and so chooses not to call home and confirm the plans. This decision is made out of simple laziness and narcissism. Nothing prevents the husband from calling except his trivial activities in the hotel room—watching some TV, doing a little reading, etc.

When he returns home, the house is empty. Suddenly the reality of his own selfishness envelopes him, as he imagines his wife packing up the baby and toddler and loading the instruments and sporting equipment into the car on a very cold winter afternoon. Alone in the house, he imagines her disappointment and anger towards him. He realizes—now—that he should have chosen her more immediate needs over his trivial preoccupations. He is almost afraid to see her when she returns. He can feel his own pathetic isolation, more deeply underscored by the emptiness of the house and his lonely wait for her return. The effect of the judgment made by the man is now clear and painfully real. In the wake of sin, he sees the damage done wherein his choice laid an unnecessary burden upon another and left him bereft of solace. In his sin, there is nowhere to hide. His choice has made another suffer.

The illustration I chose to make this point may seem too trivial, for some, to persuade. I think, however, that the ordinariness of the analogy (sin is like choosing self over the needs of one's spouse) carries real power to convert because it highlights the mundane nature of how we become vicious: We become vicious in the folds of ordinary choosing. In this case, we can look at the consequences of sin as the burden borne by the wife. All of our narcissism, or its opposite (self-hate), relays effects upon others. Our sins are never private, because human nature is social. We are made for one another, not for the self alone.

Also, note the emotional experience of the husband in the empty house. Even though painful feelings of loneliness may not always accompany awareness of personal sin, they do illustrate the objective effect sin has upon the vicious person. If he continues to choose self, in contradiction to the real needs of another, he *will* be alone.

Out of such emptiness, we cry a petitionary prayer. "O my God, I cry [to you]....But I am a worm, and not human" (Psalm 22:2a,6a). The words of this psalm appear much too self-condemnatory for our "enlightened" age, but do in fact reflect the authentic feelings of those who have seen their own glimpse into hell as a consequence of choices made. The real enlightened ones are those who see how deeply they jeopardize their own human dignity through sin. Once seen, they are now vulnerable to grace, change, and interior transformation. In the light of this, they can say, "I have looked long and deep at my character, and it is not healthy; it needs to be healed. Lord, heal and elevate me, so that I might participate in your truth."

The last thing we really want is to be alienated from others, the self, or God, even though we choose these quite frequently. Pathetically, we choose what is most against our dignity and nature: We choose *not* to care for others or for the self. We choose *not* to respect the worth of other people and the urgency of their real needs. As a result, we are impoverished. This kind of choosing leads to our being bitter, lonely, angry, and sad. We may not always be able to trace the source of these afflictions to sin, but barring diagnosed depression, they are born out of our infidelity to serving another in love and truth.

Meditation Room:

Do you recall a time when the effects of personal immorality highlighted sin's power to isolate you from God, self, and others?

When we bring this personal awareness of sin to public liturgical prayer, we become not only aware of our personal failure, but are oriented to the needs of our neighbors as well. The prayer of the faithful within the context of the Mass is a powerful agent for moral conversion if entered into consciously and explicitly.

When we enter this prayer, we are saying to God that we recognize *other people* with needs. This eucharistic liturgy facilitates not only communion with Christ, but as a result of such communion, moves us out of self in the strength of divine friendship, to serve those we remember in prayer. The entire Mass is a "conspiracy" of God to reconfigure our lives deep within the Son of God. Thus, within Truth Himself, we come to real integrity—an integrity that floods over into service of others and healing of selfishness. At the end of Mass, we know who we are again, and we can "go in peace, to love and serve the Lord" and one another. We come to know our identity, *not* as a goal of the Mass, but as a by-product of its purpose: the adoration of the Father in and through Jesus Christ and the Holy Spirit.

Desire

Possessing the desire to become morally good is the energy of any true moral conversion. Without this desire, there is no fuel for God to use in the holocaust of the "fat relentless ego" (Iris Murdoch, *The Sovereignty of Good*, Schocken Books, New York, 1970, p. 52). When we desire to be good, we yield our selfishness or our self-hate over to God, so as to be purified in God's refining fire of unconditional love.

The psalmist says, "Sacrifice and offering you do not desire, but you have given me an open ear. I delight to do your will, O my God; your law is within my heart" (Psalm 40:6,8). These are powerful words of desire. Do we have "an open ear"? Do we recognize the law of God "within [our] heart"? The desire to be with God, to be like God, is the core disposition to cultivate in a life of virtue prayer. To have an open ear is to have a heart or conscience that seeks to be instructed on what is morally true. Then, after the ear of the heart is open, we live the incredible reality of having God's law as our own heart. The heart, or conscience, is no longer seen as separate from God's law in the way a student is seen to be separate from the text being studied; rather, the text (God's law) fills the mind so much that the truth therein is appropriated as one's own.

What is the text of God's law? Basically it is the content of the covenant revealed in the Scriptures. It is a text that has intellectual content, of course, such as the commandments and decrees of God. But most profoundly, the law of God *is* God. In Christian faith, the Holy Spirit is the "new" law; the Spirit becomes *torah*, or God's instruction. The Hebrew people always looked upon the commands and teachings of God as signs of love. God has loved us so much as to instruct us in truth. But this instruction became even more a sign of love when it was revealed that it is God who *is* our law; in Christ, God came to be truth for us, and through his life, death, and resurrection, Christ leads us to holiness.

We have come to understand what "God's law within my heart" truly means through the coming of Christ. God loves us so much as to take up residence within us as Holy Spirit. The Spirit is the "new covenant" (Jeremiah 31:31), the new law of grace, who dwells within us and teaches us the meaning of moral virtue from within a life of faith and hope and love. We come to learn what is good because we are instructed by indwelling truth, the living Spirit of God. This instruction, however, needs to be confirmed by the Church. Thus personal prayer is contextualized within communal prayer and discernment.

Meditation Room:

The virtue of *obedience* has been caricatured lately as simply meaning doing whatever an authority tells us. Spiritually, obedience is much richer. Obedience is freely given to God because we desire to listen to God out of love. In listening to God out of love, we are obedient and free at the same time, a state that many in modern society think is impossible.

Living a life desirous of being with God and becoming morally virtuous is both gift and task. It is a graced cooperation that is fulfilled in our own seeking after meaning in life. Desire is a strong affective attraction and enabling emotion; it needs to be guarded, and ways of securing its motivating power need to be uncovered and named.

There will be times, however, when desire wanes. Then we are left with memory. *In memory, we have the helpmate of will.* We can will ourselves to say, "I do not really feel like praying or choosing virtue right now, but I know that what I am choosing now without desire was shown to be the truthful way of living in the past. Thus, on the basis of memory, I choose it again, and I know it to be true even though I do not feel it." Without the stirring of desire to become good, virtue is never internalized, and without virtue being our own, there can be no memory of *loving* the moral life. Without such memory, the moral life soon dies within us.

If, however, we do come to love God and virtue, we enter a life of rich beauty. It is beautiful because love of God and all that is good, together, constitute the very meaning of human existence. In this kind of living, we are taken into a deeper kind of awareness, an awareness born of living a life faithful to God and what is morally good. This deeper awareness can be called a life of contemplation.

Contemplation and Moral Virtue

Contemplation is the fulfillment of a desire to spend life in the presence of God. The object of contemplation, for Christians, is the mystery of Christ's life, his hosting of truth and love. The crucial theme that forms the Christian mind is one of moving beyond *any* hate—of others or of self—by a sacramental sharing in Christ's crucifixion (Mark McIntosh, *Mystical Theology*, Blackwell Publishers, Malden, MA, 1998, p. 41). By means of a sacramental entry into the paschal mystery, believers begin to be tutored in how to *host both love and truth*—even if it kills us. Of course, this kind of discipleship is *designed* to kill the ego, the selfish leanings of the person. It also—with some frequency even today—leads believers to actually die in fidelity to such hosting.

It is assumed by the Church that the moral life of believers will be deeply formed by sharing in this mystery of the life, death, and resurrection of Jesus Christ. To not be so formed may indicate that we have not fully appropriated the call of Christ. We cannot read the contents of another's heart, but we know—through the testimony of those who have *converted to Christ* and those baptized who have been *re-evangelized*—that there are "degrees" of affiliation to Christ and his Church. We *can* move from a more nominal association with Christ and the Church to levels of deep mystical communion. Our capacity to so judge is, in fact, the basis for recognizing persons who are "nominal Christians." Such conversions—from only a nominal adherence to Christ to a more mystic-centered adherence—are made possible by the summons of Christ to come and feed off the paschal mystery as the source of a living discipleship.

To live in the paschal mystery is not to live an arcane or mystified life. The most ordinary of extraordinary persons, the saints, found that their route to virtue and holiness was as close as their parish church and their vows of commitment to marriage or religious life. Since God wills the salvation of all (Titus 2:11), God has deemed to make the saving mission of Jesus accessible to all through the ordinary elements of Earth and human life as now arranged in the sacramental life of the Church.

What is going on in contemplative prayer, then, is our sustained, loving presence toward the profound reality of Jesus Christ's identity and mission as our savior. This sustained loving presence may take many forms, and yield to differing approaches, according to the individual personality of the person or group (i.e., religious order or lay institute) who is praying. The core reality, however, is never changing: those who pray and more deeply come into contemplation are forever entering the loving mystery of God's presence in Jesus Christ's life, death, and resurrection. This mystery is shared with us through the Church's ministry, and this mystery's unfolding is our destiny forever in heaven. Living such a reality impacts the mind, forms the conscience, and shapes the behaviors that follow from our obeying just such a contemplative conscience.

Above I noted that, through the paschal mystery, Christ taught us to host truth and love. What does that mean, exactly? I noted too that a person or a community is engaged in virtue prayer when the aim is to reach the foundation of all moral goodness in God. This is the kind of prayer that prepares us to host truth and love, because it connects us to our strength in God, who is our sustenance and our inspiration. To host truth and love, we at times need a fortitude beyond any temporal motivation. There are some things that our conscience bids us to do which instill fear within us. In order to live out the truth of our conscience despite such fear, a habit of virtue prayer can sustain us. In this kind of prayer, we explicitly turn to God, who is goodness itself, and ask for the strength, will, and knowledge to follow through on God's call to host love and truth. We do such hosting by way of enacting the truth that our conscience bids us to.

Meditation Room:

Fortitude is a virtue that enables us to do the morally right behavior despite our personal fears. Can you recall a moment when your practice of fortitude enabled you to be faithful to your conscience? At times, it is good to recall such occasions, and give gratitude to God for opening and sustaining you in your choice for moral truth.

To host love and truth, we must immerse ourselves in the prayerful contemplative gaze which over time renders us more vulnerable to God's influence. In this, we are built up to moral virtue despite hardship or fear or suffering, because he who we have been communing with has already passed through such hardship, fear, and suffering. The fruit of contemplating the paschal mystery, of being drawn into sharing the sacramental life, is simply and profoundly the construction of a heart configured to Christ's own.

Perhaps we can better understand contemplation and its fruits by looking at a common domestic experience between a father and his child.

There are times when a father goes about his day in almost

automatic service to his children. He picks up clothing and launders it, feeds the children, plays with them, comforts them. There are other moments, however, when this same father can become transported by the child's presence into moments of contemplation. This form of contemplation is something that *comes to* the father. He cannot plan it, but through his presence and service to the child *in love*, he readies himself for contemplation to alight upon him.

Let us imagine a father has just collapsed into a chair, after serving the many needs of his toddler during the course of an afternoon. As he rests, he notices his child sitting quietly on the floor, playing with a small toy, and the father is deeply drawn into the presence of his child. He begins to feel wonder and awe arise within him as he thinks, "This child exists only because of the love between my wife and me. Where did he come from, this boy who never existed before our married love? Who is he, really? I am so grateful for him."

The father's thoughts grow silent, and imperceptibly the child enters the heart of his father at a most profound level. How he loves this child! Contemplation on the dignity of this toddler simply *happens* to him; it nearly overcomes him. He arises to embrace the boy, an embrace that surprises and delights his son, an embrace with a source so deep that the child—no matter what his age—could not fathom, had the man attempted to explain it. And so he is silent.

From that moment on, however, the bond between the man and his child—and even his wife—is deeper, more real, more steady. He has been visited by contemplation, and its fruit is clarity of identity and purpose, a deeper union with the object of contemplation, all in a context of an increasingly quiet joy. This is what happens to us, on a grander scale, when service and love of

God open up to contemplation on God's dignity, as our creator and savior, in Jesus Christ.

In this experience of contemplation we come to host the truth and love of God, just as a father hosts the truth about and love for his child. This kind of knowledge about love can be so concentrated and intense that, at times, it causes a kind of "pain" in the heart. In this way, we feel overwhelmed by love. This pain is not usually long lasting; it serves as a means for the beloved to enter deeply into the lover's heart. We welcome the one we love into our spirit. We come to "host" this person and, in so doing, the beloved changes us. This change, or conversion, comes about through our fidelity to this beloved, a fidelity that strengthens our unity.

In the course of being faithful, the means for deepening unity are unleashed—suffering with and for the one we love and, in many cases, also suffering *because* of the sins of the one we love. We literally host, or become *victim,* for this person's presence in our life. There is growth in love and a movement away from vices *because* of such fidelity to another. We learn to withstand another's presence in their sinfulness, and through the other's goodness we know transcendence and joy as well. By this I mean that, in loving another unto his or her and our own moral goodness, we know both the pains of sin—theirs and ours—and the grace of conversion.

This is why Christianity is at once sophisticated and yet very simple: sophisticated because there are nuances and distinctions to be made in understanding how we come to know God in love and prayer; and simple because all such understanding and conversion occurs within the geography of "ordinary" love.

What, then, does it mean to host truth and love, and how does this assist us in virtue prayer? To host truth and love means to be faithful to love, which means fidelity to a *real person*. In order to *move from vice to virtue*, we must *maintain bonds of love* with some one, or some community, and that one or that community, in turn, must be faithful to us. Such fidelity is the matrix of growth in knowledge of self, knowledge of other, and knowledge of God.

Not all levels of fidelity demand the same self-giving, of course; friends cannot demand as much as spouses. But any kind of fidelity can be painful, and so, in a life of fidelity, there are times of temptation to break bonds, to leave a relationship, to "give up." The pain of fidelity can make a relationship seem like we are simply "enduring" a presence, with little or no joy of union. Here we are at the core of the mystery of Christian living. We are, at times like these, asked by our faith in God to draw the strength needed to endure this suffering from our immersion in Christ's life, death, and resurrection. Then we truly begin to live "by faith, not by sight" (2 Corinthians 5:7), or any other sensate proof of consolation.

This reality of living the paschal mystery, is not simply an object lesson from New Testament history, but *a power* to be drawn from and lived out of in the current moment. Of course, any suffering that we are undergoing as a result of fidelity to love has to be in accord with the great commandment, to love God and to love our neighbor as our self (Mark 12:29ff). We are not asked to endure the sin of another unto our own self-hate (e.g., being abused by domestic violence).

This pattern of faithful love is the pattern of virtue prayer. We are called to be faithful to God's love and the invitation to be in God's presence even unto our own ego-death, unto the eradication of selfishness. Such eradication is a foundation for our decision making. Fidelity to prayer is key. As we regularly "show up" for prayer, we are asking God to come and abide with us. In prayer, we want to host the divine love and truth within us. We desire to surrender so that we might be transformed, converted from sin, and eager to attain holiness. We want our prayer to form us in virtue, to gift us with dispositions to act on behalf of moral goodness.

This kind of transformation takes fidelity. We know that God will be faithful to us (Matthew 28:20). We know that God is always accessible to our prayer, even if we do not effectively enjoy the divine presence. God is still there, even if we do not "feel" God with us. We can turn to marriage again for an analogy.

On occasion, spouses emotionally withdraw from each other for healing, or thought, or simply in preoccupation with a project. The bonds of love are still there, the relationship is in place, but we still undergo an emotional dissatisfaction during our spouse's affective withdrawal. Of course, God doesn't withdraw to "think" or "do projects," but by analogy we can see the possibility of one still being bonded to another in fidelity despite a lack of emotional satisfaction. (This state cannot be indefinite, however, because over the long run it will weaken the bonds of love.)

We do not really know why we sometimes feel God's presence more or less than at other times. Some have speculated that it is because of our individual sin: We moved away, God didn't. Or is it possibly a "testing" of our love (i.e., do we just enjoy the emotion of being with God)? The point I wish to make is that believers, just like spouses, stand in fidelity despite the ebb and flow of emotional unity. We are *determined* to host this person in relationship, *for the sake of love*. This is true with spouses. It is true with good friends. And yes, it is even true with God.

The goal in all of this praying unto our own moral conversion is to come to some sustained belief in the presence of God throughout our day. We come to live what Saint Paul urged, a life of "praying always" (2 Thessalonians 1:11). Dying to selfishness and living in awareness of the presence of God and the needs of others comes to us over a lifetime of prayer and fidelity to virtue in the context of our vocation. This is not to say that some have attained such insight and holiness earlier in life. God can gift anyone, at any time, with piercing insight into the meaning of moral goodness and the capacity to live it out. It appears, however, that slow growth (and on God's part, even toleration of our sinful setbacks) characterizes the path to salvation for most of us.

Meditation Room:

What resources from our Catholic tradition can you draw from in order to remain *faithful* to God in prayer and deed, even when you do not feel the divine presence deeply?

A fine source of inspiration for us as we travel the road of moral conversion and virtue prayer is had in 1 Samuel 16:7: "The LORD does not see as mortals see; they look on the outward appearance, but the LORD looks on the heart." Significant growth in the life of virtue prayer comes when we nurture the hope that taking on the "eyes" of God is really possible. The goal of Christian moral living is to see as God sees. By this, I do not mean that we hope to be perfect in some divine way, but to simply live our lives in loving and faith-filled discernment. In a life of loving discernment, we come to distinguish between what is of God and what is simply passing or bound to our culture. Even more deeply, we hope to develop a real capacity to be able to quickly grasp what is morally evil and what is of God. This kind of transformation in our ability to discern can only occur if we change our heart, our conscience. That is, we need to read our life according to the *contents* of our Spirit-inspired heart, and not the *appearances* affirmed by the secular values of passing time. In this way, we come to see our own conscience in the light of God's way of seeing. God, in the "voice of Christ" that *is* conscience, reveals the moral truth to us, if we are open to hear.

If, as Samuel says, the Lord looks into the heart, what does the Lord see there? That is a question which is almost too much for us to bear at certain times in our lives. We feel a burden of inadequacy, due to sin or complacency or simply the busy-ness of our lives. We are not very reflective about our actions, or even our omissions. We know we can become *more* aware, *more* contemplative. *We know this*. We *can* form a conscience that is born from the depths of our attentiveness to God in prayer and to the ways of faith-informed reason. In prayer, we *do* want to know the settled presence of the Holy Spirit in our heart, a heart that the Spirit reads at the deepest of all levels: truth and love.

Do we really love the truth of moral goodness? Do we really love God? In our haste to not confront such embarrassing questions, we rush to answer, "Yes, yes, of course." To even raise such questions is seen to be impertinent. "I worship God, attend Mass, pray my prayers. How *dare* you ask such a thing!" But beyond an immediate habit-like response to such a piercing question, the Spirit will search *all* the folds and caverns of our hearts and reveal the truth about ourselves to us (1 Chronicles 28:9; Psalm 11:5; Proverbs 20:27; Romans 8:27).

There is no need to fear the Spirit who dwells within our heart; the Spirit abides there, not to condemn, but to call us to name the truth about the state of our conscience and, where needed, to repent. The fear we feel about any needed moral conversion is similar to the fear we know before we go to visit a physician. We focus on the pain that will be a part of our healing, and not on the healing itself. Just the anticipation of pain prevents some of us from seeking out healing. Analogously, it is common for parishioners to not approach the sacrament of reconciliation or pastoral counseling for fear of a similar pain—one that precedes *spiritual* healing.

Saint Alphonsus Liguori taught that God dwells within us for one reason *only*: not to hurt us, but to move us to love God in return.

> *Does God love you? Love him....Your God is ever near you, nay, within you....In the morning he is there to hear from you a word of love or trust, to receive...the offering of your whole day—acts of virtue and good works you promise to engage in to please him, pains you declare yourself ready to suffer for his glory and love....At that very moment, he utters to you his gentle commandment: "You shall love the Lord your God with all your heart." During the day renew often the offering of yourself to God.*

EUGENE GRIMM, C.SS.R., EDITOR
THE COMPLETE WORKS OF ST. ALPHONSUS DE LIGUORI, VOL. II,
PP. 395, 398

The love we seek from God is waiting to be known if only we trust that God is present even in the pain of conversion, even in the pain of naming our sin, of owning our embarrassing choices to go against truth and love. In the process of praying our way through moral conversion, faith is truly needed. Do we believe that God is present to us even in the pain of owning our sin? If we can believe this, we can get through the pain of moral conversion, and begin to know the happiness and freedom of living in virtue. But in order to reach that place of happiness and freedom we need a much deeper life of prayer, a life of intimacy with God that, in itself, will fuel the movement from sin to virtue—and without which, temptation to sin will revisit with agonizing regularity.

Conclusion

In this chapter we entered a meditation upon the meaning of virtue prayer. Understood more as a way of living, and not simply prayers said for our own moral conversion, we come to see the power of living out of our soul. This power is divine in origin, and implanted within us upon baptism. In our baptismal identities we are grafted onto the glorious body of Christ. From within this relation to Christ, we draw the power to eschew vice and love virtue from the power of the Resurrection.

Resurrection power is not engaged by simply remembering Christ's own Resurrection. Rather, it is engaged by participating in this mystery through the sacramental life. This life is not arcane, difficult to find, or elitist. It is a life to be known within the distance between our home and the parish church, between the parish church and those in need. Moral conversion occurs when we lovingly participate in the self-offering of Jesus upon the cross and his Father's response to that act of love in raising Christ from the dead. We too can hear the Father's voice raising our dead conscience to life, if we truly hand over our listening heart to the truths uttered by Christ in the doctrines and worship of his Church.

CHAPTER TWO

Rediscovering the Soul Through Prayer

A mericans are somewhat embarrassed by the idea of having a soul. As "rugged individualists," we are not ready to journey there; we know it as the doorway to the divine, as the weak point of our human constitution. "Come, O Lord. Break into our individualistic leanings and help us see that without you we are nothing." Those words do not come easy to many of us. We do not like to pause around the weak points of human control and independence; we prefer to be lulled into thinking we are alone in this universe—that even if there *is* a God, that God is distant and acts simply to maintain "the system."

We cannot fathom that such a God wants to enter the nooks and crannies of *our* life; neither are we sure that we *want* such an intimate God! We have been told that *we* are everything. We are wealthy Americans, knowledgeable, certain, perpetually optimistic, and educated in letters and ingenuity. We are needed in this world…we think. Religion makes us feel, well, un-American. It makes us feel *dependent* upon Someone.

Until and unless we come to a point where we can let the cultural myths of our American identities go, we will never become religiously contemplative. We will have a great deal of difficulty finding the soul, the doorway we open to let God in, if we really believe the goal of our popular, political, and economic culture is to simply make our life "successful."

There really is a spiritual way of living, and some attain it. As seekers of truth, we should like to be among their number. I remember speaking to a seminarian who was telling me about his summer work in a very poor section of Mexico.

He was working in a small village, teaching English as well as helping out the families who lived there with household chores. One day he went to the "shack home" of a woman he was meeting for the first time that morning. He stood in her doorway, and she motioned for him to come in. When he entered, he immediately noticed the lack of furnishings and material goods. He did, however, see a painting of the Sacred Heart of Jesus upon the wall.

"What a wonderful painting of Christ," he said to her. "Yes," she responded, "Christ is my Lord."

"I am an American seminarian. I have come to visit your village this summer, to help out where I am needed. May I help you in any way?" She looked at him very kindly, and said, "I have no needs that you can help me with."

"Surely," the seminarian continued, "I can send you some furnishings or other supplies."

"No," she reiterated, "America cannot help me. Jesus is my Lord."

All sorts of ideas raced through the seminarian's mind: "Perhaps she doesn't understand my poorly-spoken Spanish, or she is somewhat emotionally or mentally confused. I know I can help her in some way." What was most astonishing of all was that this student could not get her out of his mind for months afterward. Here he was, offering her the help of many good Catholics in

America, and she rejected this in favor of her life in its present condition. Why would anyone do that, he wondered?

After he related this story to me, he said, "You know, I think she was the first person I had ever met who was truly living out of her soul, truly unimpressed with anything but her relationship with God. I also have to say that my American pride was hurt as well. Imagine, we have all this stuff in this country and someone actually refused to take it, refused to take what we take so seriously."

When we search for, find, acknowledge, and live out of our soul, what kind of life results? It may lead us to refuse material support from good-willed missionaries or it may lead us to *become* that good-willed missionary; but most of all, it will ground our very life in the living God. In so living, we come to see life in the light of God's loving care for us, and *what we want* will *be less* because *who we have become* will fill our days with meaning and happiness. This kind of happiness is the end point of our moral and religious conversion, not its starting point. We can only hope to become like that poor woman in Mexico, not in mimicking her freedom by imitating her outward lifestyle, but in discovering how to "live out of the soul."

Meditation Room:

Have you ever met anyone who "lives out of his or her soul"? What is a characteristic that person has that moves you?

Material self-deprivation does not, in itself, result in the discovery of our own soul. In fact, poverty can embitter us and turn us from God. Only in beginning to move away from sin do we get to the soul. Once there, however, a further struggle ensues.

The battle to move away from sin is real…too real. It manifests itself in temptations, rationalizations, defensiveness, anger, and at times in defeatism. That is why willing our self out of sin is not the prescription for happiness. Left to our own power, we cannot help but fail.

Some of us, when we reach this state of helplessness, say wryly, "I cannot help myself." This statement is simply made to whomever is listening. It is acknowledging a fact about who we have become. A person who is struggling with gluttony or lust or greed begins to face up to how vice has deeply taken over the choices he or she makes. In fact, Catholicism recognizes that we, indeed, cannot "help ourselves," but need instead to reach out to God, so that grace may assist us in breaking the habits of sin. In order to develop a life wherein fatalistic attitudes over our weaknesses do not prevail, we need to see that a life based upon drawing power from grace is the *normal* life of discipleship—a life of learning to live out of the soul.

Living out of the soul in prayer is really the beginning of all Christian and moral virtue. It is the beginning of virtue because in turning to prayer, to the soul, we go to the *source* of all goodness—God—and thus have anchored our moral conversion to the most powerful and sustaining strength known. In so doing, we can withstand the winds of temptation, and even resist despair at our lack of "progress" in virtue. Such strength comes from listening, not to voices of "success" or competition or envy, but from listening to the voice of Christ speaking about our own conversion directly, simply, and truthfully within the soul.

What Is the Soul?

What can Catholicism teach us about the soul, this place of contact with the living voice of the Holy Spirit?

According to the *Catechism of the Catholic Church* (CCC), the soul is "our innermost" being (CCC 363), reflective of our dignity as being made in the image of God. This image is simply our being self-knowing, self-possessing, and therefore capable of freely giving the self away in communion with others and God (CCC 357). The soul is our spiritual center. It is not opposed to the body but, in fact, works to integrate the spirit and body in a unity of virtue. Only moral evil is opposed to all that is good about being human. Our soul is what animates our body to form one living person destined to live forever in God.

When we recover our soul, what is it that we have found? Quite simply, it is the deepest aspect of our self, that which makes us uniquely human. In finding our soul, we have found the route to self-conscious living in the presence of God. We have, in other words, found "abundant" life (John 10:10).

I use the words, "found the soul," not because we really lose *our capacity* to commune with God—that is always a part of our makeup—but through sin we lose our intimate loving friendship with God until we repent. After repenting from sin, we can come to know God again in deep love because that is *always our purpose* as human persons. Nothing can remove our nature from us. That is why we always have hope. We trust in the promises of God because we realize that those promises have our welfare at heart. The promise of the grace of salvation is always there for us; we were, in fact, created to receive such a graced promise. Truly, nothing can separate us from the love of God (Romans 8:39) except our own rejection of that love. But even our rejection does not stop God from loving us; it simply stops us from loving God.

What I mean, then, by "finding the soul," is our discovery of our identity as the image of God. "Yes, I can have intimacy with God, and not only *can*, but am *called* to, by my very nature as human." Finding the soul is finding the truth about who we are as free, thinking, loving creatures of God. It is simply being who we are and letting God be who God is *for* us. To live a soulful life is to live out of the very truth of our humanity. It is to live out of our freedom to love the truth and other persons *in the grace* of Christ's saving mission. To find the soul is to receive the indwelling presence of Christ and, in grace, to be healed, elevated, and enlightened with wisdom. To find the soul is to find the very meaning of life.

It is, then, crucial to discover the soul. It is paramount to recognize those things that can cause us to lose our way. These are the things that make living small and self-centered. Particularly, we can lose sight of the soul through much busy-ness or its opposite, sloth. Sloth is a vice that robs our enthusiasm for living. It is a hopeless state of thinking "nothing really matters," particularly our own actions. In sloth's worst form, we actually despair over the goodness of God, coming to think that we can never become good because God is so much more perfect than we will ever be. In this, of course, we forget that moral goodness is not an "achievement," but is a gift from God. Life can become small for the individual believer, but the Christian community stands as a witness to life's largeness, to its transcendence.

The way out of sloth is the way into trust in God. It is a trust born of prayer, a prayer that gently reminds us that God is not expecting perfection, but only the happiness we gain through loving obedience to God's word. We do not need to be perfect. We only need to know that immoral behavior can be forgiven, and in light of such gracious mercy we move toward grateful living as persons who are so loved. Thinking that we can never live the moral life because we are "not good enough" is truly the beginning of despair, not realism. More realistically, we ought to receive the graces needed to live the moral life as faithfully as we can, never despairing at our vices. This is true because we continue to hope in the promises of God, in Christ, who will never abandon us in our common mission to build up the Church in virtue.

We are true moral agents, free to choose what is virtuous, but we need spiritual assistance. We have to come to believe that "not everything happens on earth." Ironically, it is through deep interior living that we come to a profound transcendence. In other words, we go deep into the soul in order to be led out of the self to a life of solidarity with God and all friends of God who live in virtue. When we truly discover our soul, there is no concern over becoming too introspective or solipsistic. In fact, when we truly discover the capacity for intimacy with God from *within,* we set about living a life that reverences God through all that is *in the world* as well.

When we go into the soul to find God, we in turn are invited out—sometimes experienced as an unrelenting call—to attend those who are in need. This is true because dwelling deep within the soul is the Holy Spirit. Our Christian moral life has power because it is *God's nature* to be *for* others. We, who are *taken up* into God's life through the sacraments of the Church, are then *turned out* to meet the welfare of others. As a result of our baptism, which is the coming of the Holy Spirit, we are forever turned toward God and God's world in love, if we cooperate with grace.

The Indwelling Spirit

What does it mean to have the Holy Spirit dwelling within us? Saint Bonaventure associated the presence and work of the Holy Spirit with the purifying of our conscience *(Soul's Journey into God*, Paulist Press, New York, 1978). This purification is needed so that we might see clearly what is good and true. It is not enough to simply turn inward, to embrace an interior life. We must also discern which ideas and patterns of thinking within the conscience are of God and which are not. The Holy Spirit helps us because we cannot know the mind of God, only the Spirit can (1 Corinthians 2:11). We can distinguish between the soul and the conscience by simply acknowledging that the conscience is the soul when it makes a decision about good or evil. The soul is related to conscience, or "heart," but the conscience is the soul in its capacity to decide for or against truth and goodness and, therefore, God (CCC 368). Thus, the Holy Spirit teaches us about God's ways from within a purified soul. Listening to and obeying in action the voice of the Spirit purifies the soul. Listening to and for this voice, however, needs to be done in the context of Scripture, Church teaching, and spiritual direction by one's pastor or other qualified minister.

Normally, we do not experience the direct voice of God. We know God's voice as one that works through the truth that we detect within our mind, a truth that is the fruit of theology, prayer, worship, Scripture, and the lives of the saints.

Meditation Room:

Honesty is a virtue that holds love
for what is true in highest esteem.
In what ways do you listen for what is true?
When the truth challenges you, how do
you avoid rationalizing or excusing
yourself from its claims?

The first place to turn for the purification of conscience is the Word of God. This can be done in private reading at home and through careful attention to the proclaimed Word of God during the Mass. Of course, as we grow in the desire for an interior life, both attendance at Mass and the private reading of Scripture increases. This increase is assured, as we come to see worship and the Word as the spiritual doorways through which we pass to enter a life of virtue prayer. The interior life, founded upon worship and knowledge of Scripture, inevitably leads to service of the needy, as discussed above. The Holy Spirit, who we attend to in prayer and meditation, guides the development of virtue and the purification of conscience.

Servais Pinckaers notes, "The work of the Spirit is to enter within us by touching the two deepest chords of our hearts, the affinity for truth and the yearning for goodness and happiness" (*Morality: The Catholic View*, St. Augustine Press, South Bend, Indiana, 2001, p. 85). There is dynamic interpenetration between our interior life and the Holy Spirit who uses the things of this world to teach what is good and true. The mode of this teaching is not dramatic in and of itself; we are taught gently, through thoughts and feelings. We do need to *learn* to attend to these inner promptings of the Spirit in our conscience, however. The place to *learn how to listen* to the conscience should be the parish; the place to *practice what one has heard* is within the ordinary activities of daily living.

Today, we truly need to turn our parishes into spiritual life centers. I cannot go too deeply into this topic here, but the roles of priests, deacons, and lay leaders need to become more spiritually-centered in order to enable parishioners to recognize the work of the Spirit in daily life. Without this leadership, the spiritual life as the foundation for Catholic moral life will not be seen as practically relevant. (See my and Anthony Ciorra's *Moral Formation in the Parish*, Alba House, Staten Island, New York, 1998.)

Let me give an analogy of how this teaching from within the soul is experienced. One day I was having lunch with a friend. He ordered a healthful salad with boneless, skinless chicken strips, and I ordered a hamburger and french fries. We were talking pleasantries when the full picture of what was happening before me suddenly became clear. My luncheon friend was a vascular surgeon, someone who sees the results of my lunch in his patients' pathologies every single day on his operating table. He didn't caution me about my lunch, or lecture me, or even joke about it. He simply ordered a salad. He *said nothing* about my choice from the menu, but everything *he did* spoke reasonably against my choice.

These thoughts coalesced in my mind within an instant— surgeon, salad, burger, fries. I knew that what I had chosen was not healthful. In a combination of witness and internal promptings, I came to see that I had to change my lunch choices.

This example is about food and diet, and even though there is nothing *intrinsically evil* about eating a hamburger, it touches upon morals. We can analogously insert our last sin or vice in the place of the hamburger and get a pretty good idea of how the

Holy Spirit may prompt our personal renewal. (I am not discounting that eating healthfully can also be a moral issue.)

There is, in any work of the Holy Spirit, an internal prompt, an idea, a feeling. This prompt is usually stimulated by an external action, or by the action of the mind thinking about an immoral act, a temptation. There will be a response to this situation or idea from the indwelling Spirit, in the form of our own thought. "I wonder if I should keep thinking this way....I wonder if I should proceed with this activity." These questions are simply that: questions. We still have to discern the truth. We have to converse with the Spirit, with truth. We have to distinguish between what actions or ideas are good for us, as disciples, and what actions and ideas may be morally harmful. We also have to distinguish between feelings that may be carriers of truth and wisdom and those that are simply neurotic burdens.

Such distinctions may come clear to us after a time of meditation, or they may have to be brought to a friend or spiritual director, sometimes even both of these, and possibly in combination with a psychological counselor. All of this assistance is still the Holy Spirit trying to help us. For example, is our mental wrestling with what to leave our children in our will based upon justice, or perhaps residual anger against one child and favoritism toward another? It may not be self-evident, but due to an acknowledgment of internal promptings or questions we need to work through the idea and come to a moral resolution. This "working through" is bathed in the Spirit to the extent that we are vulnerable to becoming prayerful in the process of decision-making.

The key, however, is to begin to attune our heart to the motions of the Spirit. The discipline needed is listening: learning to listen, both to words from the soul and from external situations. On the occasion of eating lunch with my surgeon friend, the act of distinguishing good from bad was immediate as a result of a thought-informed image: "I am eating a hamburger and fries with a man who saves the lives of similar dieters every day. What is wrong with this picture?" From that picture or mental question/image came the truth: "Your diet is unhealthy, change it."

I remember counseling a recent convert to Catholicism, during which he recounted his "moment of truth" in similar photographic images.

I was stealing money from my old business. One day I was withdrawing money from the bank at the drive-through window, money I had stolen from my work, and caught a glimpse of my daughter's smiling face in the back seat through the rearview mirror. All of a sudden the words, "Your daddy is a thief," came to my mind. I knew in that moment that I had decisions to make about how I was living my life.

The truth coalesced around an image: father as thief, daughter as joyful trusting innocence. What is wrong with this picture?

In these coalescing images of the mind, the indwelling Spirit is calling us to truth. The drama of life is whether or not we begin taking the steps needed to respond appropriately to such a call, whether or not to begin our moral conversion. We speak about missed opportunities or wrong roads taken. Our choices are real, and unless we begin to choose virtue, the missed opportunities and wrong roads can seal our moral character as vicious.

This moral awareness needs to be practiced within small or incidental moral moments, not just in large ones like stealing money from work. In fact, if we do not practice moral awareness with small matters, we will be able to rationalize the greater vices *with ease.* An example of how the Spirit works on small vice will paint a clearer picture of the listening skills needed to convert from greater immoralities.

I was in a store recently to buy a small alarm clock that I'd noted was on sale. A clerk told me that there are other clocks also on sale in a different part of the store. I picked up the clock I was looking at, and went to look at the others. Finding one more inexpensively priced, I was thinking of leaving the first clock there—on the wrong shelf.

After a moment, I changed my mind; I decided to return the first clock to the original shelf where I had found it. Why? After I'd removed it, the shelf was empty; someone looking specifically for that clock in response to the sale circular would be unnecessarily frustrated to find an empty shelf when, in fact, the store had one clock. If I left it in the wrong place because it was convenient for me to do so, others would not be able to find it.

Now, as my children might say, "What is the big deal?" A store clerk would round up the clock and put it back where it belonged so someone could purchase it. That may be true, but it misses the real point. The inconvenience experienced by the clerk is not the wrong done, since someone could have left the clock in the incorrect location inadvertently. The clerk has a responsibility to return it to its proper place, so that *is* no big deal. The "big deal" in this small morality tale is that I became aware of my vice—laziness—in the light of having empathy for others, even empathy for so slight a matter as inconveniencing another customer who looked forward to getting a bargain. Once I became aware of my vice, I had a choice to make: compound my leanings toward sloth by ignoring the empathic image in my mind, or discipline myself by walking the clock back to its original shelf in the first department I visited.

It is a small matter indeed, but still I felt a tug in my will to *not* let go of my sloth. That is, I felt a desire to not choose virtue because the virtuous act I was contemplating could be labeled as inconsequential or optional. But is it really "optional" for those who want to "put on Christ"? For Christians, Christ *is* virtue. By that we mean that in Christ is *all* the variegated levels and textures of human goodness, both small virtues and large.

To be honest about our own weaknesses is essential for growth in holiness and virtue because the triumphs of the will in small matters give the faith-informed mind and will *practice in choosing the good*. This kind of practice builds upon our character; it readies us to do the good eagerly in the future. It also makes the mind and will supple in response to more difficult invitations to virtue, when more is at stake.

My description of the thought process that came upon me in the clock aisle is more complex than the actual experience. The idea to return the clock to its proper aisle simply appeared to my mind; there was no angst or obsession with the idea, there was no great struggle. Two important points, however, arise for meditation. First, even within this simple act, which called for me to walk only three store aisles away from where I was standing, I recognized a desire to *not do it.*

Recognizing this puts the whole of moral conversion in perspective. If we know a tug toward vice in little things, imagine the excuses and rationalizations we invent to avoid greater duties. Second, despite this perceptible tug to say no to a small act of justice, the decision to cooperate with virtue was, in the end, rather easy. This is obviously true because the matter involved was so slight, but it is also true because there must have been some habit of virtue already within me.

I think my eagerness to do the right thing came from two

sources. First, as noted above, saying no to sloth in this case was rather simple and so, even for a slothful person, overcoming the temptation would be "easy" (just what slothful people live for!), and therefore attractive and do-able. Second, and more substantive, is something that has not yet appeared in my scenario: the role of faith in Christ.

Why is it necessary to bring Christ into this lightweight example of selfishness overcome? Because, after our being claimed by Christ in baptism, he truly wants to think *for us*, wants to infuse our minds with wisdom from the indwelling Spirit. Is the indwelling Spirit really concerned about a clock? No. But the Spirit *is* concerned with both my moral good and the welfare of others. The moment my moral imagination started to think of the needs of others, I knew the Holy Spirit had been operating; I knew, at some inchoate level, that what I would do in yielding to the temptation of laziness was not "Christ-like."

That vision of disciples being called to imitate Christ is lodged deep within my faith-imbued mind, and it operates to call me and all disciples to virtue, even in circumstances involving light matter. The call is not a heavy sense of dread, or of being driven by a neurotic conscience, but simply the realization that what I was about to do should not be done and could be left undone for the benefit of another. I was simply practicing who I was and wanted to be, someone who, *because* Christ has claimed him, thinks of others' needs. Present in the Christian soul is *that kind* of thinking, that kind of mental connecting between some actions in a department store and the meaning of discipleship.

A goal is to have such a connection grow even stronger and make us more sensitive, so that through grace Christ will be *thinking in us*. Successfully developing such a faith-filled moral sensitivity is true freedom. The more we participate in the life of taking on the mind of Christ, the more we are liberated to be who we long to be: Christians. It is, in fact, doing immoral acts that weighs down the mind, making us heavy and sluggish in doing the good. We are only truly free in eagerness to do the good. This eagerness develops the more we live a life of discipleship, a life centered upon Christ, a life that bears fruit in thinking of others first out of love for self and God.

Does this kind of thought process always occur, always work and bring us to the same "others first" end? No, but the reason is *not* because the Holy Spirit of truth doesn't prompt. It is, rather, because we do not respond in a similar generous and just fashion. And that is because we *choose* to not respond in such a generous fashion. Therein lies the danger of letting little matters slide. Such sloth leeches into the bones of our character, and hardens our responses to moral goodness. After a while, we cannot move toward the good so easily. After a while, we may be unable to move at all.

Meditation Room:

**What does it mean to say that
Christ thinks within me? To say such a thing threatens
my own identity, does it not?**

In discussions on popular psychological principles, it is common to hear warnings about "imposing" moral norms on other people. It is said that we ought not listen to what others tell us should or should not be done, but should discover these norms on our own. We are warned to not begin sentences with "I should…" or, worse, "You should…." Some counselors are afraid that this kind of language bespeaks a neurotic approach to decision making. By that, they mean that the word "should" may indicate that a person is being confronted, not by moral truth in the Spirit, but is simply pathologically driven or pathologically confronted by another.

The Holy Spirit does not make a person feel *driven*. The truth that comes from the Spirit is firm and persistent, but can be welcomed in peace, so as to be thought about and understood. Any disproportionate sense of anxiety or urgency about what the soul is being taught may well be a sign that emotional healing is needed before we can see moral truth clearly. This is why mental healthcare can be seen as an ally to moral truth-finding in the Catholic tradition, not an interloper. Christ wants us fully healed and integrated—emotionally, morally, and spiritually.

Alternately, however, there is need to caution some popular interpreters of psychological principles. The mere fact that we say, "I should not do…" or "I should not think…," ought not to assume neurosis. By itself, the feeling that we should refrain from certain acts does not necessarily reflect an unhealthy state of being neurotically driven. The conscience *can indicate* that we should not do a particular thing, and thereby the conscience is *cooperating* in our mental and moral health. In fact, when we are healthy in mind, soul, and conscience, "should" and "should not" are messages of liberation, not of affliction.

The Virtues of Christ

If we want to discover our soul, then, we need to be prepared for an intense journey. Going within the soul is an encounter with the self, with the indwelling Spirit, and with the truth between these two. If we have been at odds with the moral truth in our ideas or actions, that encounter may be painful. The Church has given us a place of healing, however. That place is the parish, in its celebration of the sacraments. The sacraments, especially Eucharist and reconciliation, are powerful spiritual medicines for the healing of the soul, even a soul that may have long forgotten truth. (Saint Bonaventure, *The Works of Bonaventure*, Vol. II, The Breviloquium, Paterson, New Jersey, 1963, pp. 223-226.)

To remember truth, the soul needs to become welcoming of God approaching in Christ and his teachings. The desire to pray and to be virtuous is a response to God's approaching us with the beauty and truth of divine being. As we more readily rise to the occasion of virtuous living and to prayer's never-ending welling up within us, being good and being prayerful become the rhythms of our life. They no longer stand as goals to be met, but life orientations to be maintained.

In our American culture, we tend to set off in our own direction to accomplish, achieve, "make our mark." We initiate many changes. This desire to initiate can be good; it can even reflect the truth that we are made in the image of God, a God who is supreme initiator and creator. God wants us to share in this creative impetus, and gives us the world as the place to "co-create." There is, however, a caution attached to all our initiating. We can begin what God does not want us to start. We can, due to our lack of contemplation, start off in a direction that is simply of our own choosing. That direction can be a sinful one.

To initiate moral evil is *our* doing. During terrible disasters we tend to ask, "Why does God let this happen?" After the terrorist bombing of the New York World Trade Center on September 11, 2001, Catholics at a local parish asked their pastor the same kind of question. He answered their question in a homily that took the focus off of God and put it squarely on his questioners.

*Why do we choose to live this way? Why do human be-
ings choose to do evil instead of cultivating a society of
love and justice? The power to choose the morally right
act is in our hands. God gave that to us. Instead of us
asking God questions about his involvement in evil, I
think God is going to have some questions for us!*

If the power to do good is in our hands, we are also painfully
aware that we need to tap into the divine power for assistance in
accomplishing that same good. As we long to grow in Christian
virtue, we come to realize that we must share in the virtues of
Christ in order for our virtues to be long-lasting and fruitful. One
of the truths about Jesus' life was his earnest practice of the virtue of obedience. He only wanted to initiate what his Father had
willed for him. His was a life of self-emptying and humility. To
be humble is not to be passive; it is to be directed by truth.

Having our actions and dispositions directed by truth is certainly powerful, creative, and fruitful. To know what the Father
wills for us, we, like Christ, must listen deeply to and see clearly
into the things of God. We need to learn to love *silence,* so our
hearts can hear truth. Learning to love silence is contemplation.
In this silence we come into the presence of the one who is truth.
And we need to behold *beauty,* so the eyes of our minds can be
purified. Beholding beauty is wisdom. In this, we receive from
truth what we need to know about loving the moral life. We come
to love the beauty of the truth, and its beauty molds us into wise
persons. Both truth and wisdom come from dispositions of prayer,
humility, and the practice of moral virtue. They come, in other
words, by living a life of sharing in the virtues of Christ. The
source for this sharing is the sacramental life.

We have, of course, the dangerous option to forgo obedient

living and simply "go it alone" through private initiation. Private initiation is different from prayerful initiation; it is based upon *me*, even if I have consulted with others. The initiative was generated *by me* and sustained *by me*, and the credit or blame is taken *by me*. Not all such initiatives fail in worldly terms, but all such actions are self-enclosed.

For believers, initiative comes only as an obedience. Over time, we come to want to listen to God, rather than to the self. This is prayerful initiation. We seek not only consultation with "experts" but we pray, and we endeavor to listen to the voice of God's poor ones. Such poor ones may be very close: our children, our spouses, our friends in Christ. To live a life of prayerful obedience is not to live as if we "cannot think on our own," nor is it a life devoid of common sense. These are the stereotypes given birth to by those who claim to follow God with abandon but instead just do silly things. In obediently adhering to contemplation and wisdom, we try to discern weak foundations for initiatives—such as pride or greed—from strong foundations that question whether this act is going to further the mission of Christ, or serve the poor, or help the common good.

This is not an extra layer of decision making, tacked on in awkward fashion because we "believe in God." Rather, it is an approach to decision making that becomes second nature; it flows out of the very character of those who are becoming "a new creation" (2 Corinthians 5:17) through contemplation and wisdom. After a time, we simply become discerning and obedient initiators. No drama, no big show. We simply come to think with, in, and because of Christ. From small decisions, like putting sale clocks back in their correct aisle, to large decisions about family, business, and political life, no initiative is done in a solitary manner. All is filtered through the only reality that will last forever: communion with Christ and others.

In the sacramental moral life of virtue prayer, we are "caught up" in the life of Christ (Mark McIntosh, *Christology From Within*, University of Notre Dame Press, Indiana, 2000, p. 117). In this life of being caught up in Christ, two gifts are bestowed: the gift to truly plumb the depth of who we are, for without Christ we would surely go mad from the twists and turns of our own sometimes tortured souls; and the gift to live with others, for without Christ we truly could not endure the presence of others—nor they, ours—in hope. We could *tolerate* one another's presence, and maybe even have *pleasant conversation* and do *some service* to and for one another, but it would be difficult indeed to reach the depth of intimacy and fidelity called for by Christ when he bid us to love one another. The spiritual stumbling block to such goodwill between us is sin.

How does Christ help us plumb the depth of our soul, and how does he help us endure one another's presence as we oppress and are oppressed by sins?

Knowledge of the Soul with and in Christ

The revelation of who we are *in ourselves* is the gift of Christian discipleship. In order to come to appropriate our true identity and dignity, however, we have to pass through a confrontation with our illusions about the self. A false sense of the self needs to be healed or reordered or wholly rejected, depending upon the depth of its hold upon us. As in the transforming encounter Simon had with Christ in order that he come to see himself as Peter (John 1:42), so too will we be brought into our new identity in Jesus.

The knowledge of our soul, of who we are in our capacity to "know" God, comes through an *encounter* with Christ. There is no other way for the disciple to discover the self *as disciple*. We can come to know the soul through an encounter with the moral truth, but this is simply an encounter with Christ waiting to be named, for all truth shares in him who is truth itself. So, whether knowledge of our dignity as God's beloved comes explicitly through Christ or implicitly through an encounter with the moral truth, we need to cultivate such encounters for sustained growth in the moral spiritual life.

This growth is not some descent into meditation upon the self, but a growth in holiness, a meditation and activation of the self in relation to divinity. Of course, the self is not swallowed up by divinity; we are not *absorbed* into God. Just the opposite, in fact. The more we give ourselves over to God in Christ, the more we come to a secure sense of the self, a self that is meant to be given away in love and service. Thus the encounter needed to reveal our soul is not esoteric or mystified, but local and domestic. It is as close as the truth uttered by our spouse or our child, and as local and "ordinary" as daily Mass celebrated in our parish. It *has to be* this mundane and close, because our salvation is at stake; anything more difficult would be elitist, and beyond the capacity of many people to usefully pursue. Salvation—the knowing and healing of the self in relation to God—is *always* close at hand (Luke 10:8-11; 17:20-21).

So encounter is how we discover our soul, and encounter is quite specific. To encounter Christ, we have to be dispossessed of the self, caught off guard, perhaps already on a search for truth. That is why we can speculate that some Pharisees in the New Testament never discovered their true calling as Christ's disciples: They always encountered him in full possession of themselves, guarded, in control, almost manipulative (see John 8:9). The proper disposition for encounter is simplicity. In simplicity, we attend to and are eager for communion with God and others. "Truly I tell you, whoever does not receive the kingdom of God as a little child will never enter it" (Luke 18:17).

My two-year-old son, Liam, is not a simplistic child, but he *is* simple. He is bright and eager to meet people, and even introduce others to his brothers and sister. Liam is continually gazing up to others with an open face and smiling mouth. His disposition is simply, "I am here and wonder if I can know you, and you, me?" Being two, he obviously does not utter such words; instead, his whole being is an invitation to and a seeking for the other. I have met forty-year-old men and women who have the same simplicity: hospitable, inquiring, excited about learning and knowing, interested in others' lives and ideas. These persons are "alive"; they have encountered and have been encountered because they are open-faced and inviting of truth. They know they have a soul, and they live out of it!

How does Christ help us to live out of our soul? In what can be a long process of conversion, he replaces our fears and self-delusions with what our mind and heart have been longing for: the truth. In Christ, we come to love the truth about ourselves, the world, others, and God. We come to see that only Christ is truth, and we allow him to fashion our interior life into one of freedom and joy. Over time, and in the context of sacramental living, we come to live out of the reality that Christ *makes sense* of all things, including suffering and love, and that in those instances where the pain of love and suffering make no sense, Christ *helps us bear* all mysteries in him.

As we invite Christ more deeply into our soul through prayer, service to the poor, and sacramental living, we realize that he is changing our disposition and our outlook. We are renewed with him and in him and through him. Since we now know that the truth within us is Christ, who for the repentant is only love and mercy, we can begin to truly live life as a child, open-faced and inviting of truth.

Meditation Room:

In your religious *imagination*, what does it mean to think of yourself as a child before God? Why do you think Christ invites us to meditate upon the image of a child as the only inhabitant of his kingdom, rather than the full stature of one who is an adult?

In Christ, who unleashes the power for us to live out of our soul, we gain a "second innocence." We come to trust more in God, not in a naïve way, but in a way that reveals the journey we have taken through the crucifixion of sin and the resurrection of grace. We truly become "wise as serpents and innocent as doves" (Matthew 10:16). In the life of virtue prayer, we acquire wisdom only in conversion from sin, a wisdom graced with gratitude for having come out on the other side of cooperating with evil not only alive, but alive in Christ (Romans 6:11). And to be alive in Christ is to bear all things and know all things *in him*. This is soulful living, and the gift of Christian faith.

In hosting love and truth in a life of virtue prayer, we come to discover a call *deep within the soul*—Christ's voice calling us to love virtue and serve others. In listening to it, we grow in virtue and empathy. Christ may also *call us to the soul* by means of the events of everyday service to others. Either way, we find both the soul and others in the context of a saving relationship with

Christ. The way Christ calls us to live in full reality with others is to *strengthen the soul*, and the way he calls us to know and endure the truths of our soul is to *form strong communities of support* to assist us in bearing the journey inward.

In this mutually interpenetrating call, there can be no romanticizing of the parish community. We are not dead yet. We are not in heaven. The family, the parish, the neighborhood are filled with human finitude, limitation, and sin. The parish, however, is also prime ground for grace to work its way in us. Christ emboldens us to live together in the parish by the discovery of our soul. Living out of the center of who we are enables us to endure the presence of others, because from within our discovered souls we find our dignity and destiny in Christ together. If Christ has found us in our searching and met our search with his mercy, then we can be available to others in their search and meet their finitude and sin with compassion. We have a memory of being met with Christ's mercy, and so have no right to dismiss another as unworthy.

Despite this memory, we still do on occasion dismiss one another. This kind of dismissal may be based upon the fact that we hold only partial knowledge of the other. God holds full knowledge, of course, but the community holds fuller knowledge than any of us alone does. Over and over again in life, I have found that someone whom I have dismissed as "unworthy" is presented to me by others as kind, virtuous, and worthy of friendship. I knew a "part" and dismissed; others knew a "part" and embraced. In Christ, who knows all, we can come to be welcoming of all, in the memory of our own merciful encounter with the Savior.

This does not mean that we will be intimate friends with everyone, but, in grace, at least we can come to not gossip, slander, or belittle another. We do not know the full person. Where there is need for another to change his or her ways from vice to virtue, we can name that fact—if prudence allows—and still retain a respect for the person simply because of his or her humanity. We do not have to undermine another, for that serves no truthful purpose; it is an act of sin.

Conclusion

In rediscovering our soul, we come to the very foundation of the indwelling Holy Spirit. By living out of our depths, we can become a strong moral presence in public. When we go within the soul, with and in Christ, there is no danger that we will linger there to inspect and delight in our own ego, for Christ gives us to ourselves only so that we—like him and in him—may give those very selves away in service to the needy. The joy of such living is that, when we give ourselves away out of the strength of being in communion with Christ, we come to possess both Christ and the self with renewed vigor—a communion that is deepened within the kinship of other believers in the parish and in our family. On good days—in the parish community and in our family—yes, we can almost see heaven!

CHAPTER THREE

Conscience: Listening for Truth from the Mouth of Truth

In the discovery of the soul, we subsequently have entered the reality of conscience. As was said previously, they are not to be equated but do exist together, with conscience being that aspect of the soul which makes moral judgments. The conscience is both ordinary and mysterious. Due to its nature, we may think it is too confused or too undeveloped a reality to be helpful in moral decision making. We might argue, "Let's keep it simple and say that the conscience is simply *me* making a decision." That is not wrong, but it is an incomplete expression of Christian conscience. In the conscience, understood as the judging mind imbued with the indwelling Spirit, we come into mystery. This is so because, within the conscience, God is communicating to humanity, or more specifically, to each human person with a moral judgment to make. God is not just communicating *any* knowledge, but *precise* knowledge about a moral judgment that lies before a *specific discerning person*. The mind of this person has been readied to attend to the voice of God, echoed within the conscience, over years of loving and heeding that voice.

The more we have loved the divine voice, the more eager we are to respond and act upon the word of truth detected in the judgment of conscience. Out of the depths of this kind of mind, the truth about where moral virtue lies is more readily accepted. In this communication, we are at the heart of virtue prayer. In obediently listening to the judgment of our faith-imbued conscience, we come to its mysterious center. It is mysterious, not because the conscience as an idea is constructed on fuzzy thinking, but because, in the conscience, we enter a meeting place between self and God. There is no exaggeration here. Since the Holy Spirit dwells within us, and this same Spirit longs to communicate its holy presence by directing us to all that is good and true, we enter a sanctified territory.

Unfortunately, when we enter a place where both divinity and humanity intersect, our human temptation is to dismiss one or the other reality as not really being there. Some would then say the conscience is simply our human mind, that the conscience is the self thinking about what is ethically right or wrong; or, alternately, that the conscience is God, and we, as human, are or can become *an aspect* of the divine. These are old errors which regularly arise in human history when we get tired of living in a world not of our own making. The Christian truth is that God dwells within us as Holy Spirit, and each individual person continues to exist and thrive in communion with this holy God. The two are in communion.

To cope with this mystery, we do not need to exalt one and diminish the other; we do, however, need to learn the life of virtue prayer. We need to sit with this mystery our entire lives, and in so doing, become faithful to it and learn its content of truth. On occasion, we need to rest in the fact that our life constitutes a mystery of divine/human communion. From this rest comes all our wisdom, and the strength to know and do what is virtuous.

How do we live this mystery fruitfully, and not simply reluctantly? By "not reluctantly," I mean without a disposition that looks at this mystery as something to "crack," to figure out. "I am just not smart enough now to do it, but someday I will be, and then I will know what is really going on inside my conscience." Faith tells us that this mystery is not a stopgap answer for the under-educated, but is *the mystery* that *exists now* and will be *ever unfolding* into eternity. At our center is God. Due to this common center, we are one under a common Father. This divine/human relationship *is* human existence, and embracing this relationship is the very core of our happiness.

The heart of a life of virtue prayer is this: to become attuned to God's promptings from within the soul as the Spirit tutors the mind to take delight in the true judgments of conscience. It is a life of deep interiority with no disproportionate introspection, because the Spirit who is speaking within is always pushing us out to the world beyond the self even as it includes the self.

In order to live such a life, I will suggest a few points of practical reflection.

1. ***The life of virtue prayer is not a new vocation, but a purifying of the one already lived or the one God is calling us to.***

This indicates that we have only to look around at the life we are presently living and ask what duties born of our relationships ought to be deepened. Virtue is developed, not by willing to be virtuous in the abstract, but by acting in fidelity to the *duties present* in being a spouse, a parent, an employee, a disciple. The life of virtue prayer bids us to listen more deeply to the fruits of our interactions with all who are vitally present in our respective vocations.

It is very difficult to wake up on any given day and say, "Today I will work on the virtue of courage." More realistically, we become courageous or just or chaste in the fulfilling of vocational duties that lie within each day. For example, in order to be a good father I need to confront a truth that is blocking my relationship with my son. The energy to become virtuous is unleashed in the desire to be true to who I am as "father." In this context, virtue can develop naturally rather than being willed as an end in itself. Willing virtue as an end in itself can tend to appear as another "task to do," rather than the very meaning of our life. The urgency of one and not the other is readily apparent.

2. *Christ is speaking within.*

Beyond contextualizing virtue development within our vocation, to believe that Christ is speaking within our soul to facilitate this development is crucial for entering the new life of virtue prayer. Without this core belief, we can be swayed to and fro by *outside* slogans, ideologies, movements; and swayed from *within* by moods and dispositions that reflect only superficial aspects of the personality.

Most crucial of all is coming to see that deep interiority is assisted by deep communal participation. The more interior the wellspring of our decisions, the more communal we become. Parish life, spiritual direction, family life, and "fraternal correction" are the essential matrix for going deep into the interior of the soul with Christ. We, therefore, measure our interior growth by our communal participation and identity. Alternately, we measure our communal participation by how well we have come to discern the interior "voices" that prompt decisions.

This does not mean an introvert becomes an extrovert or an extrovert becomes introverted in order to find the "true self." It does mean, however, that both kinds of personalities root their decision making in a *conscience publicly formed*, and *in a community that reverences individual conscience* as subjectively ultimate in authority. In the end, Christ is speaking within, but all who truly hear this voice regularly confirm it with the voice of Christ that is known in the Church "where two or three are gathered in my name" (Matthew 18:20).

3. *Moral conversion from vice to virtue can occur over a period of time of forming, reforming, and listening to conscience.*

Moral conversion is a process. It begins by becoming *aware* of the vices we participate in and progresses by establishing the *desire* to be rid of them, all in the context of *listening* to the ecclesial Christ within the conscience. After this awareness has overtaken us and this desire gains roots, we live our Christian vocation and our personal vocation with new vigor and delight. The rest of our life is spent both by going deeper into virtue and by staying on guard against any reoccurrence of interest in former vices, even those that were small and hidden within the folds of our heart. In fact, after we clear out the more grave vices, we shouldn't be surprised to find a new awareness of smaller evils within us. We have hope that, in living within the sacramental life and serving the needs of the poor, these smaller vices will be overcome or managed as well.

All moral conversion is to be sustained and understood within the mystery of Christ's life. We gain access to this mystery by our sacramental participation, Scripture reading, and service to those in need.

Recently, while visiting a chapel at a Catholic university in Ohio, I noticed the well-painted and realistic Way of the Cross that hung on its walls. While meditating on these panels, I began to think about how these depictions could be used to assist us in meditating upon how our moral conversions are supported by the power of Christ's paschal mystery. It is spiritually useful for us to imagine our own progress toward the death of the ego, so as to be in concert with Christ's own death on the cross. In this meditation, we cry out to Christ to encourage us to take up a life of virtue and relinquish our vices, just as he went to the ultimate self-surrender out of love and obedience to the Father.

Of course, not everyone has a devotion to praying the Way of the Cross, but the meditation itself is found within the very heart of the Scriptures and the Mass, so is really a central one for all Christians. The acceptance of our own physical death and death to sin with Jesus, out of obedience to the Father's love and goodness, is every Christian's destiny. How might such a meditation progress?

The Stations of the Cross and Our Moral Conversion

The *first station* portrays Jesus being condemned to die. In this station, we can imagine our own judgment about our particular vices. We stand in the light of judgment, a judgment unlike Jesus' before the tribunal because ours is true and deserving. In the judgment of our own vices, we begin the journey to ego death, that death to selfishness that is essential for any virtue to be brought to life. We begin to see that our lives do not consist of simply choosing what is convenient, expedient, and entertaining. We need to come to terms with what is *other* than the self, what is *more than* our own desires. In acknowledging this, we also come to see that the self is not threatened but rather fulfilled. Initially, this truth about our present need for conversion may not be joyfully welcomed, but it must be welcomed for any joy to be long lasting. In truth we know that vice must go and virtue must be taken up. Selfishness is condemned to die. When we come to know this truth, we are not far from salvation (Mark 12:28-34).

Meditation Room:

What is the most difficult vice that you ever overcame
or are overcoming? Why did this vice linger
longer within your soul than others?
What does your faith in Jesus Christ give to you
in the struggle to overcome sin?

To continue in our personal moral conversion, we can gain more strength by meditating upon the *second station* of the Way of the Cross. In this station, Jesus is seen carrying the cross that was just laid upon him. The initial stage of our journey toward ego death is surprisingly heavy and painful. We may even be tempted to give up the journey. We had no idea that conversion would entail a real suffering, in the letting go of vice, in order to trust in the promise of an as yet unseen and unknown life of virtue.

In the *third station*, Jesus falls for the first time. The weight of our sin is heavy for him. The weight of our new journey toward virtue is heavy for us. And so, even on the way to conversion, the memory of past vices becomes too much to bear and we give in to our old ways, our old habits of vice. We fall with dramatic weight. We begin to doubt. "I guess I can't change."

Jesus is going to fall two more times, in the *seventh* and the *ninth* stations. Here we have a Savior who can empathize with us. He calls out to us to get up like he did, to keep going toward our destiny in a dignified life of graced virtue. Even if we fall two more times, we know the truth of moral goodness. We know it is our true call, and we will keep heading for it.

In the *fourth station*, Jesus meets his mother, who grieves over his suffering state. We also may have people who are grieving for us, but not in the way Mary did. We may have people who are grieving for our past life of vice. "What have you done?" they ask. "Are you a religious fanatic? Why can't we have fun with you anymore? You have changed." This kind of grief is more like that of the soldiers who taunted Jesus while he was upon the cross: "If you are the Son of God, come down from the cross" (Matthew 27:40). "Come down," they yell to us. "Do you think you are better than us?"

Paradoxically, we have afflicted them with a grief. In this paradoxical suffering, they mourn our conversion from sin because it is understood as a threat to them. "If the one we used to enter vice with has changed, why is it that we do not change too?" It makes fear rise in them to various degrees. In the end, our meeting them upon the way of our cross may be met by their eventual conversion as well, or they may simply dismiss us and see us no more. The way to virtue is not a "popular" route.

In the *fifth station*, Jesus is met with help from Simon of Cyrene. Here, after we have been undermined with misplaced grief about our conversion, we are finally given some support. At our side we find friends in Christ praying for us, supporting us with words and actions. We find the example of the saints. We find our cross lightened, as we come to see that others have trod the way we now walk toward ego death. "Perhaps," we begin to believe, "with this kind of help, I can make it out of vice and its memories, into a life of virtue." We cannot make the journey from sin to virtue without the support and witness of our faith community. We need to cling to friends of virtue during this dangerous journey, one with so much at stake.

In the *sixth station*, someone is present who actually wipes our face, who cares enough to lessen our suffering, even in a small way, without tempting us to give up the journey. There is no longer a voice of temptation, but simply a presence, sustaining us and giving us strength and comfort without removing the cross of our conversion. "Thank you for loving me enough to not take the cross of my own change away from me."

In the *eighth station*, Jesus is seen comforting the women of Jerusalem. Here we see the remarkable strength of Jesus in his ability to think of others' needs in the midst of his own walk to Calvary and death. In our moral conversion, we too may be called to serve the needs of others even while wondering from what source of strength this compassion will come. "My whole life is changing. I am preoccupied with my own concerns, my dying ego. What will this change bring, what will my new way of living cost me?" Yet the coming of others in need is simply the relentless flow of life. We do not partition our lives off; our lives are integrated into the flow of life's rhythms. We may lament, "When is there time for *only me* if I am truly open to grace, change, conversion in Christ?"

Jesus himself hurried across the lake to be alone, and simply found the needs of others waiting for him (John 6:14-16,22-25). Therefore, we try to be available to grace in silent retreat, a grace so needed for conversion, and yet, like a good monk in prayer, we rise at the knock on the monastery door. Christ has come in another form, and we are to deepen our conversion by attending to the visitor's needs. In so doing, we find that this visitor was not a "distraction" on the way of the cross, but in fact its very form. We learn that the crucifixion of the ego—all moral conversion, in other words—is about yielding the selfish self to the other in love. Meeting another's needs on the way toward holiness *is* the way of the cross.

In the ***tenth station***, Jesus is stripped of his clothing. In order to surrender fully to love in the face of evil, we need to give all. This surrender is humiliating. We want to defend ourselves, protect our reputation, our "public face," our "dignity," but to lash out against evil plays into evil's hands. So we stay centered on truth, and witness to goodness by fidelity to its ways of self-surrender rather than the destruction of others. Perhaps here is the most difficult station. Here is the beginning of the *real pain* of crucifying the ego. What we want to do is turn and run, turn and deny the truths that have led us to this point.

The price of conversion is coming clear, and the cost is claiming us. Is there no one who will cover us? Is there no one who will tell evil to stop in its relentless efforts to take everything from us? Or is it following truth that is taking everything from us? We cannot really tell from this perspective. As we lose all that we thought we possessed, as we lose all that we thought defined us—our old ways, our old life—what do we have? Is this a stripping for death and burial, or is this the nakedness of new birth? We cannot tell right now. We are afraid. "I cling to your decrees, O LORD; let me not be put to shame" (Psalm 119:31).

The ***eleventh and twelfth*** stations bring Jesus to the nails and wood of the cross. "Now the pain is beyond belief. Now I have nothing left to give or offer or bargain over. I am spent. Take me. The struggle with evil has cost me, and yet I am coming to see that, if I had chosen not to meet evil with love, my very being would have been swallowed up. What I have left I give to you, O God." The purification is now complete. The move from vice to virtue, from sin to cooperation with grace in fidelity to the human identity, has run its course.

What is next? We cannot see. We only know that, despite the pain of yielding our sinful habits to love and truth, we have not been unfaithful. We went forward to see what love demands and truth unveils. Now we entrust ourselves to you, O God of love and truth. What is left?

In the ***thirteenth and fourteenth stations***, Jesus knows the peace of death. After the struggle and pain, we yield and come to know peace. After being tested by the call to moral conversion, we feel like we want to rest. Becoming good takes a lot of energy, while yielding to temptation feels so easy, so effortless. In grace, we have struggled to no longer steal or lie or take control of things. In grace, we have tried to de-center the ego and put God in the center. We are tired now. We want to rest, and we are hoping that in the rest God will visit and make the completion of the journey to virtue smoother. May Christ fill us with eagerness to embrace the virtues needed for our vocation. "I want to look upon the life of virtue with joy now, Lord. May I not have to struggle so hard. That is virtue's reward, is it not God?—to know the delight of being good, and in so knowing to know the joy of your presence? Right now, though, I want to rest…rest in truth, in you, in the love of goodness."

The ***stations are complete***, but the reality of Jesus' mysterious walk to Calvary is not. The reality of such fidelity to his Father's word is breaking forth in new life. The moral life is the resurrected life; it is the life of sharing in the power of Christ's Resurrection. That which we thought of as dead is now alive—but alive in a way that is new and unexpected. This is not the previous life, but life lived with a new mind and a new will. We long now to think like Christ, to act like Christ—not as some mimicking play, but from within a mind transformed and elevated.

Some may not see us as new. Others may view our moral conversion in cynical terms or meet it with sarcastic words. But this change is real; we are not the same. The indwelling Spirit has affected us, and now we sing out with the psalmist, "Oh, how I love your law!" (Psalm 119:97). We now love what we once thought was wrong, stupid, burdensome, and simply irrelevant. This is real resurrected life: We love being good and want to be good forever.

For those who are still suspicious, or see these sentiments as quaint, we ask you to look again at the way we walked. We ask that you follow the same path to moral wisdom. There is nothing quaint or sentimental about wanting to be good and choosing what is right. That kind of living demands that the ego dies first, and even more may be asked of us later. To live morally is to live courageously, but in so doing we are helped because we live out of the power of Christ's Resurrection. To live out of this power is to have the mind and desires transformed.

> *Therefore we have been buried with him by baptism into death, so that, just as Christ was raised from the dead by the glory of the Father, so we too might walk in newness of life.…But if we have died with Christ, we believe that*

we will also live with him....So you also must consider
yourselves dead to sin and alive to God in Christ Jesus.
ROMANS 6:4,8,11

The Catholic moral life is one of newness. We have been healed and transformed *from within* our soul in order to cooperate with virtue, with Christ himself, who is all and every virtue. In this kind of living, sin is dead and we live now for God.

We know, of course, that not all of our desires or actions will be immediately aligned with moral goodness. There will always be a *remainder* factor from the days of living without Christ, and temptation will visit again, in old or new areas of weakness. But this is not to say that we do not make real and abiding progress in virtue out of the power of the Resurrection. If the Father can take what is dead and transform it in Resurrection, God can transform our souls to live for what is good.

To live in such *hope* is the essence of resurrection ethics. It is a hope that is desperately needed today, when many think their behavior is "neutral" or without consequence—and so seek no mercy—and some think that the power of resurrection is not for them—and so remain in a debilitating scrupulosity. Because sin is real and God has power over it, we can come to see that actions are formative of the soul, and yet also see that God can pull out those sinful roots through forgiveness. Neither cavalier notions holding that actions mean little, nor the paralysis of disbelief in God's real mercy have the last word. There is only one last word: *Christ was dead and now lives.* This word is the one that changes our life of sin into a life of virtue.

Conclusion

If the Resurrection is that powerful, and such power can be accessed even today through the Holy Spirit, what does such a life of virtue look like? It looks like the lives of the saints, the lives of those who have lived from within the soul while remaining conscious of their own ego crucifixion. They live lives of gratitude and expectation. If God can move us from patterns of sin to participation in resurrection living, what else can God do for our lives and the lives of our families, parishes, and cities? This kind of living is our heart's desire; it is what we were made for.

Meditation Room:

What is your clearest memory of change in your moral life?
How do you apply that knowledge or experience to
conversions that are needed now and in the future?

CHAPTER FOUR

Conscience: Forming a Mind Eager to Know Moral Truth

The resurrected mind is a conscience that is open to new words, new truths, new ways of judging actions. This is a mind that carefully deliberates over any moral action that confronts people of faith. This mind gives us surety and humility because this mind is following the indwelling Spirit as it inhabits both the individual and the Church. To make a conscience judgment out of resurrection power is to make such a decision out of a center of peace. Moral theologian Brian Johnstone has written that the Resurrection was a "nonviolent act." It took what was torn apart, rejected, and killed—Jesus Christ—and knitted him together again in love, grace, and creative power. After baptism, all of our reasoning powers to discern, love, and choose what is good are to be at the service of such a nonviolent power. The conscience is about finding *peace in truth as we know it*; it is not about tearing us apart in indecisiveness. In order to know such peace, we may have to pass through a turbulent time of decision making. We know, however, that as we go deeper into acts of faith, hope, and love, moral decisions will become clear and we will know peace.

It is important to realize that these decisions may or may not be surrounded in emotion. As we head toward a resolution of any ethical dilemma, and moral truth claims our mind, we may come to an answer with little or no emotion, joy or relief, but simply a resolution, "I know the truth now." We come to a place of mental rest, and acknowledge that a decision has been made so as to move on with our lives. If, for other choices that come our way, we experience joy or relief at our decision, it is good to remember that the *emotion is not* the point, *the decision is.* The desire to be grasped by truth is the goal.

How do we prepare our mind to receive the message of moral truth?

Meditation Room:

Are you aware of ever relying too heavily on emotion to confirm a decision while spurning the facts or well-reasoned arguments? Our thinking is to be informed by emotion, not replaced by it.

We prepare our mind to receive moral truth by attending to God in prayer. For believers, this may appear as self-evident. Since it can so appear, however, we may come to miss its depth. Prayer is the foundation of *all thinking* out of faith, hope, and love. If we are not praying through our decisions, and having others pray for us, we are simply relying on the resources of the secular mind. Truth *may* be apprehended by the secular mind, but it is so grasped at the expense of *intimacy* with God, at the expense of deepening our friendship with God.

As a married man, I can make decisions that are correct as a result of counsel from teachers or ministers, but if I do not engage my spouse in such a process *I have neglected a privileged point of intimacy* for sustaining love. I can get to the truth without consulting my wife, but this knowledge is gained outside of the wisdom and union of spousal love. Not only that, but a certain quality or fullness of truth may be missed because I intentionally avoided speaking about impending decisions with my spouse.

If we are baptized and live now for God in Christ, to neglect communication with God in making moral decisions is to be similarly deprived of intimacy. Over the years, holy people grow to a point where they "pray always." In such persons, an intentional act of prayer may not be as necessary in moral decision making since their virtuous living has made knowledge of truth ready at hand, almost intuitive. For novices on the journey to goodness, however, a sustained and intentional conversation with God about the formation of conscience and the decisions before us is vital. God changes our mind, God fills our mind with the Holy Spirit. The Spirit instructs us and inspires us to listen to the judgment of truth as the mind knows it. And this decision making is all done out of the faith of discipleship, our true and abiding identity.

I will share an incident wherein the necessity for prayer in moral decision making became clear to me.

I was visiting a church in Massachusetts during vacation one summer with my family. As we settled into our pew, I began with my usual personal preparatory prayers for the beginning of Mass. The entrance rites passed and the Liturgy of the Word began. After the Gospel, the priest began his homily. He had a booming voice. He underscored certain words with dramatic inflection. I began to make a swift judgment, "This preaching style is not so good, too showy." Then I began to listen to the words, and stopped being distracted by his style.

Suddenly a small sentence that he uttered seemed to fill the church with meaning and envelop me in peace and wisdom. The words were, "Who are you living for?"

"Yes," I thought, "Who am I living for? Certainly, I cannot go on living just for me."

I began to imagine what sort of life it would be if I met each person with the intention of living for their needs and not my own. It seemed like an exciting life, a life of growth in holiness and virtue. This was the answer to Christian discipleship: to live for others.

You may be thinking, "Of course, that is the answer, it is self-evident, and all Christians know this. What is the big insight?" The big insight is that on that morning I *knew* this truth of our faith more profoundly than ever before. The big insight is that *grace* had elevated my mind and heart to receive the truth from within the prayer of the Mass, and from within an ordinary homily that on many other days I would have ignored. I stopped judging the pastor's style and listened to hear the truth he was speaking. The truth came in a strong way. It came with intellectual power and, in this case, with emotion. I was moved from within, even as I was not moved by the homilist himself. The Spirit was instructing and I was listening.

The question of who we are living for became a guiding meditation for me after that. It kept me on track and made my will more pliable to the needs of my family and others. Having this phrase in my memory was not due simply to my powers of recollection. It has stayed with me because of the circumstances that drove it deep within my heart. It came to me in the disposition of prayer. In the Spirit I received the truth and remembered it, not because it was true, but because it was *truth delivered in love*. It was truth known in prayer.

Meditation Room:

Can you think of a time when you became acutely aware of a truth because it was delivered in love?

Truth delivered in love is a good summation of the whole Christian mystery. Jesus, who is truth, comes and offers himself for us out of profound love for his Father and for his needs. When truth is delivered in love, it gets our attention; it helps us to receive it so that such truth can abide deeply within us. As we welcome the truth at our deepest levels of conscience, we can then welcome it again and again through memory. Truth takes up a home within us. We no longer are threatened by it, or defensive about its message, or interested in self-deception and rationalization.

Once we accept truth delivered in love, we look to be confronted by truth regularly. As we grow in holiness, that is all that we can tolerate: lives of truth. The saints grow impatient with charlatans and those adept at posturing. Saints want truth because they know that such reality binds them to God in love. Truth delivered in love is what constitutes the contents of the Catholic conscience.

As we go deeper into the paschal mystery, our mind is configured to the mission, death, and resurrection of Christ. We begin to see the purpose of our life as being "another Christ," sharing in his mission, and drawing life out of service to others and death to our own egos. This kind of living changes the way we think. It unleashes a deep cooperation in and through grace with the ministry and mission of Christ. To have a resurrected conscience is to have a faith-imbued mind that more easily judges moral truth in accord with the symbols, signs, and images of the

Church. The conscience then can be understood as a moment of judgment within a whole way of thinking as disciple.

We are not simply Christian in our moral decision making, but also in our worship, our service, our prayer, our work, our relaxation. Through grace, and participation in the sacramental life, we become persons who want to know Christ in the full dimensions of the paschal mystery. We want to live deeply within this mystery as *our* life's meaning. We know we can draw life from such a reality, because it is nothing more nor less than Christ present among us in Spirit, truth, and sacrament. In welcoming this mystery into our heart and mind, we welcome holiness.

The conscience, in its capacity as the mind judging right and wrong, is the point at which both reasoning and praying coalesce. In the judgment of conscience, we accept the truth as it has claimed us, and we therefore stand before God who is all truth. Here, in this moment of judgment, is both a moral decision and an act of prayer. When our conscience makes a judgment about what is true, we come into the presence of God. We know this is a correct understanding of what is happening because to disobey the judgment of a well-formed conscience is the very definition of sin. In the judgment of conscience, we grasp the will of God as best as we can any particular judgment, and thus this act of judgment becomes a simultaneous act of rapt listening to God. To raptly listen *to God* in the manifestation of the mind's judgment of what is true is, in fact, *an act of prayer.*

The Second Vatican Council confirms that the judgment of a well-formed conscience is an encounter with God, albeit implicit. The doctrine of our Church is clear: For those who *do not know Christ,* salvation can be gained by following the judgment of conscience; for those who *do know Christ,* to turn away from the conscience is to sin—to turn away from God (CCC 84, 1849). In the practical realm, then, the conscience is the doorway to the sacred in the sphere of personal ethical decisions. To listen to and follow the judgment of the conscience is a holy act, and attention to a correct formation of conscience is crucial so that we may show reverence to the same indwelling Spirit of God who chooses to speak to us there.

Both the formation of conscience and the skill of moral discernment are key to reverencing the dignity of conscience. What is "formation" and what is "discernment"? To form the conscience, we have to be aware of three things: *who we are*; *where we learn about moral truth*; and *who we go to with questions about moral decisions*.

The first question is answered by our baptism. We are Christ's. We are therefore Christian. It is Christ whom we listen to above all other authorities. It is from him that we gain our identity, and it is to him that we look for moral direction. All other secular and cultural authorities are to be regarded as only more or less helpful in clarifying the meaning and purpose of our life.

Christians learn about moral truth most explicitly from the community to which Christ has given his Spirit: the Church. We are obliged, in love, to go to the Church—with its worship, its doctrine, and its saints—first and foremost. In most cases, this dialogue with our own tradition will be sufficient to form our conscience in fidelity to our baptismal identity. Our identity is truly and fully known *only* in the light of our love for Christ in the context of the Church.

There are, however, some contemporary moral questions that—in order to be answered truthfully—may need a wider context from within which to find an answer. This might be seen in some issues of healthcare ethics, genetic research, politics and religion, prudent approaches to modern war and terrorism, and so on. Not every moral question was answered at the time Scripture was written, nor at the time past doctrinal formulations were developed. The Holy Spirit continues to teach the body of Christ about new issues that arise in every generation. In order to answer moral dilemmas wisely, Catholics must attend to the proper secular sources to gain the wisdom that only they can share.

We need, finally, to discern the moral truth for us in our unique circumstance. In order to do this, we need to go to our religious leaders. Usually this will be our pastor. If that is impossible for varying reasons, another priest or other expert in Catholicism can serve us in our need to come to moral truth. The reality of discussing our immediate moral decisions with a religious leader is crucial in order to confirm what our conscience is judging to be true. In this way, we get external and objective confirmation about what our conscience is judging subjectively. It is not always necessary or possible to get external and objective confirmation, but whenever some doubt lingers in our decisions the virtue of prudence obliges us to do so.

There are many wise persons in any given secular culture to whom we could go to get counsel, from newspaper columnists to professional counselors. The emphasis I place upon religious leadership, however, should be clear. We are making our decisions *out of our baptismal identity,* and so we give to our priests, deacons, and religious a presumption in favor that they too love our faith-filled identity and will guide us accordingly. This assumption cannot be as reasonably held if seeking advice from secular leaders.

It is particularly disappointing when religious leaders are said to give little import to church doctrine while wanting to appear "open or tolerant" or even "with it" regarding the spirit of the times. Such "leaders" are, in fact, leaving their people bereft of authentic Catholic advice. This is negligence on their part, and profoundly sad. We can only take solace in its rare display.

Conclusion

As love of Christ and his truth grows ever deeper within our heart, there does indeed appear an eagerness to follow conscience. In our efforts to appropriate our Catholic identity through the sacramental life, we come to see that our mind is changing: We think new thoughts and desire new meanings to fill our days. The old vices are sloughed off, replaced by an eager longing to know what living the good life really means. In this we seek to spend time at the well of our new life: prayer, contemplation, worship, Scripture reading, and service to those in need. These then become more than answers to catechism questions regarding what makes up the "good" Catholic life. Enfleshing them through our choices and actions becomes our ardent hunger. The fruit of such a life is the liberation of living out of a Catholic conscience. Truly, our mind has been refashioned by the indwelling Spirit of Christ and, see, we are doing and thinking something new! (Isaiah 43:19).

Meditation Room:
Who was the best spiritual guide you ever had?
What qualities does a person have to possess to guide another into being faithful to a life of following conscience in peace and joy?

CHAPTER FIVE

Practical Ways of Living a Life of Virtue Prayer

Remember that virtue prayer is a cry for moral goodness based upon contemplation. Contemplation is a disposition to behold the good things of life in our heart. In order to become virtuous through prayer, we need to cry out from a contemplative heart. We need to desire such a conversion, and desire it because we have seen goodness or because we have seen our own emptiness in the face of naming sin and long to replace our sins with virtue. Either way, a cry goes up from us to God, asking God to change us from the inside out.

How should we live out a life of virtue prayer practically? I would like to share five practical ways to move from a life of vice or strong temptation to a life of virtue and inner peace. These five ways are to be approached from within a rich and deep faith life. They are not to be seen as steps or methods of achieving change apart from faith in Christ. The change comes from within a dynamic faith life.

1. *Seek prudence in prayer.*

"Therefore I prayed, and understanding was given me; I called on God, and the spirit of wisdom came to me" (Wisdom 7:7). The way of virtue prayer is the way of seeking the virtue of prudence. Like all virtues, prudence is attained through practice. The prudent can discern the voices of our age and come to rest in truth. The best preparation for a sustained life of prudence is found in the Wisdom prayer for virtue. In it, we are bid to seek wisdom above all else, and in so doing we will receive "all good things [which come] along with her" (Wisdom 7:11a). In such prayer, we are conversing with the author of goodness and wisdom itself, and so we come to live a life of moral goodness in a manner sustained by the Holy Spirit. From out of wisdom, strength is found to convert from sin in a praying heart that is vulnerable to the promptings of God.

Do we really want to be wise; or do we want to be pleased, wealthy, popular, or attain only other passing values? It is a difficult struggle to come to be satisfied with only wanting to be good. This goal is not usually culturally rewarded with accolades or material success, or even in admiration of our character, so laying the foundation for a moral life in seeking prudence from God in prayer is a sure beginning to a difficult journey.

To become prudent is to become lovingly deliberate in our decision making. In being prudent, we are not removed from any situation in an impossible quest for pure objectivity. We are not being simply cautious, or even timid, in decision making. We are certainly not ruled by political expediency. We simply seek the truth in love. The prudent are guided to moral goodness by a mind and will that have been affected by prayer: sitting at the feet of wisdom and coming to trust in what we learn in prayer, spiritual counsel, Scripture reading, worship, and the lives of the saints. In the end, we make our *own decisions*, but out of a *profound conversation* of love with God in Christ.

2. *Trust in the resurrection power of Christ for conversion.*

When listening for wisdom bears fruit in an answer to a moral dilemma, we still need the power to follow through and live out that wisdom. If we have come to see that we live an egocentric life, we still need to concretize the ways to dismantle that kind of living. We need to seek ways to say no to the self, and to listen to and for the needs of others. This kind of life pattern change is a *suffering*, and we will not go down the road to moral conversion for long if we think it is a road we walk alone.

We move ahead in fits and starts. All conversions have some backsliding. We need to commit ourselves to the goal of becoming virtuous in a certain area of life, and commit to the behaviors that direct us to that goal. And that is a commitment we must keep despite any frequent lapses of progress. It helps us to remember that all virtue is formed in us in the context of our vocational commitments and relationships. We become just by treating others fairly, not by simply saying, "I want to be just," and finding some opportunity to "prove" it. The opportunities to grow in virtue are located within those relations with others that we daily live out and the duties associated with maintaining them.

We come to live a more just, chaste, temperate, prudent life by integrating those virtues with the theological virtues (faith, hope, and love) in a matrix of living out our vocation to Christ domestically, publicly, and parochially. We need to draw from the power of Christ to sustain our journey, and to go to him when we have succumbed to temptation. In this turning and repenting, we are reconstructed anew by grace. In the story of the rich man (Mark 10:17-27), we see Jesus extend an invitation to discipleship which entails a complete trust, a foregoing of dependence upon wealth and the self alone. The rich man cannot positively receive this invitation because he cannot yield such control and power over to another, not even to Jesus. In failing to do so, the young man misses the opportunity to live life to the full.

After his refusal to follow Jesus, we are told, he goes away sad. In giving our moral lives over to Christ, trusting him to change, forgive, and renew us, we are liberated from scrupulosity on the one hand and presumption of our salvation on the other. We are freed to live the life of virtue within the context of truthful self-knowledge and the divine reality that nothing is impossible with God (Mark 10:27). In those times when our journey to virtue is not heading straight and swiftly to its goal, we can recall the power of God and let it reconstruct us from within the mystery of resurrection (new life) through the offer of divine forgiveness (healing).

God is the one creating us into moral persons. Do we trust in God to do so? The result of not doing so, of not undergoing the change that God has seen fit to work within us, is sadness. This sadness does not have to be. By surrendering unreasonable control over to God through our participation in the life of the Church, Christ *works to change us from within*. What at first might appear to be simply a call to *will our way* through moral conversion is, in fact, a call to *receive the grace* of conversion in league with our consent and cooperation.

Saint Bonaventure knew of such grace in his understanding of moral conversion.

[Saint Bonaventure] modified from within the very idea of virtue: from a habit due to personal effort, he has made of it a quality that God himself operates in us, through which, by making us like him, our acts are made proportionate to the goal of our supernatural vocation (Livio Melina, Sharing in Christ's Virtues, *Catholic University of America Press, Washington, DC, 2001, p. 133).*

3. Listen to friends and enemies who bring the truth about our character to our awareness.

News about our moral faults is very difficult to endure. Our natural reaction to bad news is denial. As we grow in virtue, we can arrive at a point in our inner life wherein we welcome critical assessments about our character. In fact, learning to listen to the truth about ourselves from others is one of the fastest routes to moral change. This is not to say that everything someone says about us is true; its veracity has to be further discerned. What we can achieve is an initial hospitable stance toward another's judgments of our behavior. Once we are open to listen, we can discern if what is said is true or not.

The desire to learn from others about one's moral status is actually found in many of the saints. They welcomed "fraternal correction," and at times sought it out, not because they wanted to hear "bad" news about themselves, but because they sought holiness with a passion. They knew they needed to live in reality about their own character in order to be affected by grace. To some extent, we could say that the saints were asking to be told what was wrong with them so that they could bring that fault to God for healing.

To seek such information about the self is not to promote a neurotic introspection or scrupulosity. Again, moral health is mental and spiritual health. Obsessive thinking about right and wrong needs to be healed. The moral life is a balanced life, and we need patience to enter it and sustain a journey to virtue. Impatience with the self over a perceived lack of moral progress simply breeds anxiety; it can lead us to give up. We never want to get so stressed out about moral growth that we come to see it as an oppressive burden. Our growth in moral living is our *liberation* from human infidelity—sin. It is a joyful journey and a "light burden" (Matthew 11:28).

To grow in the virtue of listening for truth, no matter its source, is one of the most helpful of all moral dispositions. Those who follow either the trends of the current age as authoritative or live only for past articulations of moral goodness enslave themselves to blind obedience. We are of course to listen to the moral authority of the pope and bishops, but the pope himself condemned blind obedience as beneath human dignity (*Veritatis Splendor* 42). We are to listen to the ecclesial authorities out of love for truth. We are to approach doctrine, Scripture, and worship open to hear what God is teaching. Remember, we want to be affected by God, and we know, through the promise of the Holy Spirit, that we can trust God to teach us through the magisterium of the Church.

God's truth also comes, with less communal clarity and certainty, through any other means God wills. All of culture becomes a vehicle through which God can instruct us. Can we hear God teaching us? Sometimes we cannot hear God as clearly in culture because it is the stage from which all other voices teach as well. In the light of this reality, it becomes even more urgent for parishes to become centers for moral discernment—places where people can go to work through new moral ideas and test them in the light of the Catholic tradition.

If we love the truth, we will welcome it from wherever it arises. We will not "kill the messenger." We may not like the message about how we need to leave sin behind, but that is only because we have lived in sin, or the habit of sinful thinking, for so long that we feel the truth is our enemy, a threat to our life, not the hoped for fulfillment we have been waiting for. To learn to listen to truth and for truth is a crucial disposition in moral conversion.

Meditation Room:

Recall a time when the truth about your character or behavior came from a surprising or unwelcome source. How did you react to such a situation?

---

4. *Act on virtue, even if you do not yet feel like it.*

This is the most difficult step in moral conversion because our emotional life is not yet in sync with the good we know we are called to do by conscience. After someone has offended us, for example, we certainly don't feel like being just or prudent in our response. We normally want to "get even." We ultimately have to train our emotions to derive satisfaction and pleasure *from virtue*, especially if we have been engaged in such vicious behavior as revenge or gossip over a period of time. If we do not engage in such training, we will likely not develop "a taste" for being good; the moral life will appear uninteresting, or beyond our personal reach. Think of the experience of wanting to lose weight, for example, and knowing we have to exercise, but at the gym we feel the pain of the workout—"This is a drag, I can't do this"—and so we don't go back. And we don't lose weight.

If we are to grow in virtue and holiness, there will be times when we'll simply need *to will* doing the good, no matter what psychic or emotional difficulty it presents. If we skirt this ascetical reality, the likelihood of moral growth is diminished. If we "just do it," over time the burden will be lifted, and the virtuous life will be our joy. Being good flows easily from a heart that loves being good and wills good for others.

Willing the good may sometimes be experienced simply as "an exercise to go through" at the early stages of letting go of a vice and acquiring a virtue. The exercise is contextualized within the loves of our lives, however, making the willing somewhat palatable even from the beginning. We are gritting our teeth, so to speak, out of love for another. We are moving away from anger or greed or any of the "deadly sins" because we love our family, ourselves, our God; or because we learned of our sin's impact on another. The change working its way into our heart, in other words, is not simply a "be good" principle. The change has *a face* attached to it.

Due to our knowledge of the harm we inflicted upon another, we make a turn toward virtue. The personalization of our conversion helps to speed us along with its initiation and completion, for we certainly do not want to hurt people again. Acting on virtue with a "face" in mind, a memory of a real person who suffered some level of injury at our hand, assists in pushing us to do good. In the effort to attach an affection to our move from vice and not to simply rely upon a volitional and cognitive "obeying of rules," we learn to cultivate empathy. In time, this empathy operates even at the level of memory and imagination.

A man who recently struggled with balancing his work commitments and family life noted, "I do not want to see the disappointment in my child's face again," after he broke a promise to be with his child during a particular school event. Keeping that "face" before his moral imagination helps him to better balance his duties and loves. He will perhaps never achieve perfect harmony between the pull of family and professional interests and satisfaction, but he has learned to use his moral imagination to call forth empathy when decisions confront him. This kind of progress moves ethics beyond a sheer willing; they enter into the realm of empathetic love. Love is surely the most fertile ground for the development of virtue.

5. *Be grateful to God for the simplicity of life.*

This kind of statement is not meant to evoke idealism, or to echo a sickening piety of irrelevance, but rather is a reminder that moral progress will never be made unless we actually enter into the mystery of life as being truly simple. Such simplicity is a refraction on Earth of life in heaven. Again, to meditate upon heaven is not to seek "pie in the sky" but to reject the clutter of our consuming lives, and so come to clearly see life's essence as being in communion with others. The only reality that inhabits heaven is loving relationships of virtue. The saints begin to live heaven on earth as they delve more actively into simplicity, draw pleasure from it, and come to will activities that deepen friendship in acts of love, justice, and prayer.

When the complexities of life overwhelm us, we can turn to the simplicity of prayer and see there the wedge point, sharp and thin, that allows light to stream forth—not from our center, but from the center of the Trinity in heavenly glory. The light is not as brilliant as it is in the full presence of heaven, but its refracted rays clearly turn our heads toward the needs of people—needs that can only be served by entering their presence in and through a virtuous heart.

The simple life is founded upon trust in God's salvific will. We can learn to attend to relationships in love because we believe that God has our best interest at heart and acts to secure our adherence to that selfsame divine heart. Understanding that God is acting within us for our own welfare is crucial if we are to develop a life of joy and peace. These fruits flow from a transformation that moves us from being *bound* to "this age" to becoming *bound* to God. Since baptism, we have been "freed from sin and enslaved to God" (Romans 6:22). What or who we are bound to makes all the difference in the fruits we come to know. To be bound to sin is to become disfigured and fearful, because sin can only bind us to ourselves and this age of death. When we are bound to God, we transcend this age; we enter the beginnings of an eternal life of relationships of love. God wants to give us this kind of life, even as we keep insisting on our right to make or fashion a life of our own choosing, which of course is usually short-sighted and self-serving.

Conclusion

This book has been an invitation to meditate upon the integrity of the moral and spiritual life. As we delve more deeply into the mystery of God's love for us in Jesus Christ we come to see how, from within that mystery, we are ushered out to behold the dignity and worth of ourselves and all human persons. In other words, the more we descend into the mystery of God's presence among us—through prayer, worship, Scripture, study, and service—the more we are introduced to one another in God. We and God are distinct, of course, but we are not separate; we are dependently related to God, and God is freely related to us as Creator and

Savior. For believers, virtuous living originates within the heart of our love of God.

Nevertheless, faith and ethics are not the same. They have a distinction that is objectively constant, as is the distinction between what is human and what is of God. But there is a wonderful coalescing that occurs within the life and heart of Christians, and that coalescence integrates loving God and loving what is morally good.

In order to truly listen to what is true, we need to desire to love what is true, and in the case of Christianity, to love *who is the truth*: Jesus Christ. The paradox of our faith life is this: In order to discover our interiority, we need to be in communion with others who are also searching for and within their souls. We need to discover the soul amidst others who have come to find "this age" empty and wanting. The virtuous life and the spiritual life come together in a community of interiority—persons who seek to be affected by the voice of conscience heard within. This voice, however, can only be clearly recognized as true if we raptly listen to sources from without, sources at the core of the Catholic community—the word, the sacraments, the poor in their needs, the saints in their fidelity. A life of listening for moral truth and praying for communion with God is a compelling one, for it attracts us at the very core of our humanity—a core that seeks freedom and rest only in acts of surrender to God. In so surrendering, we come to know ourselves and what is good for us. Most importantly, we come to know our destiny in God.

About the Author

James Keating, Ph.D. is Associate Professor of Moral Theology in the School of Theology at the Pontifical College Josephinum in Columbus, Ohio and a Deacon in the Diocese of Columbus. He is married and the father of four children. Dr. Keating is the author of *Crossing the Desert: Lent and Conversion* (Liguori, 2001); *Conscience and Prayer: The Spirit of Catholic Moral Theology* [coauthored with Denis Billy, C.Ss.R.] (Liturgical Press, 2001); *Pure Heart, Clear Conscience: Living the Catholic Moral Life* (Our Sunday Visitor, 1999); and *Moral Formation in the Parish* [coauthored with Rev. Anthony Ciorra] (Alba House, 1998). He serves as Editor of *The Josephinum Journal of Theology*.